Feasting

from the

Black Cauldron

Teachings from a Witches' Clan

Written and Compiled

Amaranthus

I

ISBN: 978-1-936922-87-1

Editing by Raven Womack
Front Cover image by Artist Maxine Miller
Cover Design by Ted Venneman
Book Design by Raven Womack

Printed and bound in the USA
First Pendraig Printing 2017

Pendraig Publishing, Inc
Green Valley Lake, CA 92341

www.pendraigpublishing.com

Dedication

This book is lovingly dedicated to our friend and fellow witch, Lord Shawnus Merlin Belarion, Elder Priest of the Coven of the Catta. Lord Shawnus, AKA Gary Lee Hoke, Passed away on July 1st 2015. When I first meant Shawnus I was a young man living in Pennsylvania. We became quick friends and often spent weekends at his home talking in his back yard while drinking tea. Lord Shawnus was a complicated man who tried to lead a simple (and mostly solitary) life.

Shawnus was a lifelong student of the Occult and Spirituality. Receiving all three elevations into the Coven of the Catta, a branch of Wicca founded by Sybil Leek. Shawnus was also a member of the O.T.O and an initiated priest of Anubis. In his youth, Shawnus was initiated into Vajrakilaya and Avalokitesvara, as well as receiving empowerments into Tibetan Buddhism. Shawnus and the Legacy of the Catta Coven live on in his Books and his Blog. He was a true friend and is greatly missed!

Contents

Forward

Let me begin by saying that writing the forward to a book such as this is no easy task! What words does one use when describing the working of a fellow magister? And while I'm at it, am I even worthy of such a job? Which words will best describe the author himself? Of course, the obvious choices- witch, sorcerer, and magician all come to mind. And yet somehow, they don't seem to satisfy me on some instinctual level. I guess I could sing his praises (he would probably like that), but that's not really my job here. I wasn't asked to stroke anyone's ego or feed the flames of a Geburic illusion. I was asked to write from a place of honesty concerning my opinions and experiences with the author, and so I shall attempt to do just that.

It was on a chilly Samhain night in Pennsylvania that I first meet Amaranthus, before either of us knew it, a friendship had sparked between us and soon we found ourselves hiking in the mountains, cutting herbs in the field and enjoying coffee in my sunroom during the long Pennsylvania winters which seem like they will never end sometimes. As our friendship grew, I realized that Amaranthus has a tendency to be as controversial as myself, a fact that has undoubtedly contributed to a number of acquaintances and "so called friends" having their fill of us and our nonconformist ways. And yet, we stayed our course, unchanged by the peer pressures of a community that has taken the term "Fluffy Bunny" to a whole new level (yes, you know who you are).

Some of the most memorable rituals I have attended in the last decade were held by the author of this book. Our covens would often come together to work the wheel, spin the thread and dance the dance that we call witchcraft.

Each and every time we entered the circle together, it seemed as if the rituals would get better and better. Worked to perfection by the author and his students, our celebrattions were a masterful blend of old-world craft, both cunning and calculated. Simple yet complex in ways that many rituals will never be, I have been left in awe on several occasions by the intuitive practices and the dedicated structure by which these witches practice their art.

In the time of Pre-Christianity, the witches of the old world had deep roots filled with a wealth of accumulated knowledge. These witches, hedge-riders , and village folk had a covenant with the spirits that many practitioners today lack. I believe that this book does its job in showing people the wisdom of witchcraft, a belief different from those who practice today's modern Wicca, while staying true its form, the author has given people a glimpse and a taste of what it's like to be in a witches clan. Upon reading the manuscript for this work, I immediately noticed that this book was different than anything I had previously read. With many chapters being dedicated to ancestral work, necromancy and the realm of the dead, the information given within these pages can be used to fill in the holes that other authors often leave.

With this being said, the manuscript not only felt new and different but also old and familiar in a sense that it contains things long forgotten, lost upon this era's New Age mentality that everything occult must be politically correct. Here we find out that witches truly get their hands dirty, practicing what they preach, not merely gathering books to add to their vast collections. In these pages, we learn that witchcraft comes from within. Here you will find chapters on subjects rarely written about, one of the many reasons that I agreed to write this forward.

To those of us with occult integrity, the initiation oath is often times both a warehouse of power as well as a commitment to silence. It is in that silence that the secrets of the craft are revealed to those who are ready to receive them. It is my belief that Amaranthus has balanced the work in this book, as well as any witch under the oath of secrecy, could hope to do. Here we find work that is deeply rooted in Malkuth, yet dares to gaze upon the sphere of Yesod. And it is my hope that this work will find its beauty in Tiphareth.

-Lord Shawnus Merlin Belarion, 3rd* Elder, Coven of the Catta

Introduction

My intentions in writing this book have changed over the course of its creation. Truly the book I intended to write and the finished project you are about to read are vastly different. Like all acts of creation, this work has taken on a life of its own. When I first began this project, I intended to write one book, albeit a very large book, but one book none the less. At some point during the writing of the first few chapters, I put the book down and walked away intending not to finish it. My original intent was to have this work printed privately, as a large tome, for our clan members only- a sort of reference guide of our clan's teachings. It was going to be used by those students who had reached a certain level of understanding and left for them to fill in any holes they might encounter while walking the winding way of the witches' path.

It was quite some time before I picked the book back up again and looked at it with new eyes. I wrote a re-draft of the contents and showed it to my wife who immediately looked at me and said, "It's way too much for one book!". After a long discussion, I re-wrote the contents page and ended up with enough material for three books. Dividing the work in this way would allow me to give more details in each chapter and space to elaborate on the clan material as a whole. We also talked about having the work published so that others outside of the clan could see how we function and learn some of our techniques. This did, however, present a problem. Releasing the material to the public is tricky while giving the details of our clan I had to be careful not to break the oaths of the initiation. I must retain the qualities of *Sub Rosa.*

As I sit at my desk writing the passages that have become this book, I have taken notice of a small ritual I perform every night. Before I begin my night's work, I have religiously lit a single white candle and recite a small prayer to the ancestors, asking for guidance and wisdom. Perhaps I have been seeking approval from the world of spirit to write this book? Or, perhaps the ancestors have chosen to speak through me for a short period in order for their voices to be heard once more? In either case, I have called out to those spirits of witchdom, and it seems as if they have responded.

Over the next several months I had noticed a lot of activity happening in the house. During these writing sessions, I would often hear noises in the house that were unexplained. I would often hear what sounded like doors opening or shutting when no one else was at home. On more than one occasion I heard footsteps in the next room. Another time I heard what sounded like whispers coming from behind me. Most often I would feel the ancestral spirits coming as a presence making itself known in my immediate area; this spiritual force would linger in my space making itself at home. Shortly after this, my feet and sometimes my hands would turn cold. On a number of occasions, my feet would turn ice-cold as I wrote, the ancestral candle next to me danced wildly as if the spirits were pushing me to write. During the night while asleep, I would often wake up with thoughts and information in my mind. I would feel compelled to get up and write this information down as if it was vitally important. Over time I got used to this extra help from the ancestors, and their presence became something that I relied on, driving me to finish the work.

The white ancestor candle that I used eventually burned itself out and was replaced over and over again during the process of finishing this book (and of course during the re-writing stage as well). The flame of the candle would often dance and flicker as it had that first day, casting shadows across the room on those long nights of writing.

As the years have gone on, I have noticed the inner seasons that the clan has gone through. There have been times when the clan had become stagnant and less productive in initiating new members. While many of those initiated seemed to forget their oaths, others became secluded and fell into the oblivion of the mundane world; they focused on themselves and seemed to forget the responsibilities that come with being in a clan as opposed to a tradition. However, we knew that this winter season of stagnation wouldn't last forever!

The seasons of the clan are ever changing internally, and when the metaphorical springtime came again, we found ourselves surrounded by new faces and new initiates who brought new perspectives, new ideas and in time, new rituals. As a clan, our path is still unfolding before us. While maintaining our core teachings and techniques, we are able to add new blood to the clan, thus making us a living, breathing entity capable of growth while maintaining some semblance of stability. Our clan is not based on religion as it is in Wicca, we do not worship the gods in ritual, and neither do we petition them to do our bidding. We see the gods as ancestors and place the clan's emphasis on magick, the mystical arts and the power of the mind.

Like many clans, these days we practice magick in a multitude of ways. We make use of folk magick and the making of charms from Europe and the Americas, always researching and adding old lore to our new practices. We make use of traditional tools as well as some that may be original to our clan. We follow a fairy path of witchcraft that is primarily Celtic in origin with inspirations found in other ancient cultures. Yet, we also make use of ceremonial magick and are capable of calling on the aid of angelic forces and the planetary intelligence of the universe.

While the best rituals are often the simplest, we find that there are times when other magicks are needed. While some of our workings were handed to use from the covens that came before us, we have taken to using our intuition in the creation of what we now practice. We have tried to seamlessly blend the past and the present material so that those future members will take suit with the overall design and continue what we have begun.

I have always believed that the practices of witchcraft predate the rise of Christianity. On an instinctual level, I know this to be true. Looking through history books, this becomes much harder to prove on paper. While researching the "History of Witchcraft," it always seems to me that the data collected by scholars during the time of the witch trials has always been one sided. Historically speaking, no witch from that period wrote about his or her own beliefs. Nor did any witch write about his or her practices unless they were under pain of torture. All records and all data from these periods have been compiled by non-witches about those people they accused of witchcraft thus, making history records biased and filled with propaganda.

As a witch's clan, our line comes from French descent. This makes what we practice differently in many ways from those witches who have lineage into a British witchcraft or Wicca coven. Many of our tools, mystical arts, and terms that we use are very different from those found in many of the books written today. While it is true that some tools are similar in use, they are often different in design. And those that are similar in design are often very different in use. Yet still, some of our tools I have never seen nor heard of any other coven using.

It is my intention with this book series to describe how our clan operates. How we perform our magick, what it is we believe that separates us from other practitioners, at the same time giving glimpses into the system that we use for training.

It is <u>not</u> my intention with this book to prove that we come from an unbroken line of witchcraft stretching back through the ages. In truth, I don't think that is either possible or reasonable to attempt, and in my opinion, I don't find it necessary in order to validate my work, nor anyone else's. Rather, I would teach or ask, those who read forward to listen to their ancestors' voices. Listen to them, for they are calling to you from within! For it is from within, that we find true witchcraft calling to us.

1

Witchery

I have had many people over the years come to me and ask about witchcraft. Some of these individuals want to know what it is we witches do? Others want to know what a witch is. During the course of these conversations, I will often use the term "Witchery." Some people will ask me what I mean by this, while others I think just assume it is a word synonymous with witch. The best way that I might describe this to you is to say that those people born with witcheries are not necessarily witches, but rather that they possess great potential in becoming a witch.

A person with a witchery (or quite possibly multiple witcheries), is an individual who has some gift that others do not seem to have. Over the years I have met and experienced dozens and dozens of people all with various witcheries. Most witches that I have encountered seem to experience witchery in one form or another for the first time during their childhood. Depending on the witch, these abilities can sometimes come and go without any warning. Those people who possess witcheries in this way may experience these abilities very strongly one day, only to then have it seemingly disappear for a period of time. At some point, usually, when they least expect it this ability will return. It is only after the individual accepts this part of themselves and works with the witchery consciously that it can somewhat be controlled.

By definition, a witchery is a natural ability that can simulate a spell or one of the mystical arts without the use of tools, props or training in magick. Some individuals can produce these witcheries on occasion. However, they show very little control over their personal abilities including when they materialize, how long they last or, how to make them stop. This can become a lifelong pursuit for some of these people.

Often, it's not until these individuals meet someone who can help them, that they will gain some amount of control over their witcheries. The goal of these individuals should be:
    1) to understand their witcheries
    2) to come to terms with their personal power so there is little to no fear
    3) to learn of other witcheries they might not realize they have.

We believe that those people born with a witchery are showing the potential towards becoming a practicing witch. This road may lead some individuals to stand before the door of witchcraft. Some of these people will certainly start down the road to becoming a witch, but whether they complete that journey is another story. Many of these individuals will receive some limited training but never seem to find the right teacher for them. Others will find that the timing just isn't right, or that they will be unable to make such a big commitment to learn the required skills of witchcraft. Some of these people will try repeatedly only to be disappointed over and over again. For these individuals, the path of witchcraft is new to their spirit and may take many lives to master. Some of these potentials are not meant to be witches in this life. Many of them are getting their first taste of magick and will receive more training in a future incarnation.

Individuals with multiple witcheries are often believed to be old souls, those who have probably lived as a witch, psychic or mystic in a previous incarnation. It is very likely that some witches who produce a large number of witcheries have been practicing witches in several past lives leading covens and training others. The practice of witchcraft will often come naturally for these individuals.

Most commonly, witcheries will manifest as forms of psychic ability. I am not trying to imply here that everyone who is a psychic is also a witch. Some people are born to this life specifically to be psychics, helping others along their path by giving them insights into different areas of life. Witcheries usually develop at a young age. The child will often realize that they are different from their siblings and peers making them afraid to speak about their abilities and the things they have experienced. As a child, I was subject to this fear.

At a young age, I started to have a series of strange occurrences that I couldn't possibly begin to understand. Instinctually, I knew that I was different from the other children in the neighborhood and, unfortunately, school was no different either. I remember sitting in the family room watching television with my father and my sister. We sat fixated watching the television, our eyes glued to the screen, laughing a little and having a relaxing evening at home. At some point during the show, I noticed a woman standing in the window watching us. Immediately I knew that she was a spirit. This woman was completely unfamiliar to me. As I stared at her, she seemed to stare straight back at me with her cold, dark eyes. I remember sitting still, afraid to move just watching her. After a few short moments, I closed my eyes, and when I opened them again, she was gone. The woman in the window didn't appear to me that often, but from time to time she would come and watch us.

On one unforgettable night, I fell asleep in the family room, and when I awoke, I saw the woman walking from the dining room down the family hallway. I pulled the blanket up over my head afraid to look, in my mind, I knew that she would be there if I dared to look. Eventually, I fell back asleep, but the image stayed with me for a long time after. After receiving training in the mystical arts, I realized that this was a form of witchery that some witches were born with, and that others could develop this and other skills like it. In our clan, we call this *Spirit Sight* and consider this and a few others like it to be forms of clairvoyance. Clairvoyant abilities make use of the psychic eye, sometimes called the third eye. For those people born with the psychic eye, their witcheries may manifest in a number of ways. Some witches can see the future, while others can see the past. Some of us can see the here and now, often called remote viewing by many new agers.

Another form of clairvoyance that developed for me during my teenage years was *Aura Sight*. Those of us with this ability can see the electromagnetic field that surrounds a person, place and sometimes objects. For me, auras appear as color surrounding an individual. This energy field is composed of light that translates information to my mind in the form of colors. Others that I have trained to see the aura will some-times tell me that the energy translates to them as radiation or a glow that comes off the person's body. A few of these students have told me that auras appear to them as colored mist, saying that it looks more like a shimmering cloud as opposed to the colors my mind sees. Aura sight like all witcheries may work different for each person, but often we are receiving the same information.

When asked, most witches that we have encountered in the past decade have claimed to be empathic. While there are actually two distinct forms of empathy, as well as a few subcategories, we consider them all to be forms of clairsentience. There would seem to be a mass awakening of individuals who are very sympathetic souls, empathical-ly inclined to the feelings of others in this day and age. At times, it seems as if a small portion of those asked claims empathy as their witchery out of simplicity. While many psychics and witches (as well as non-practitioners) truly are empathic, it seems as if the word "empathic" has become somewhat trendy among today's modern witches.

Nonetheless, those born with empathy as a witchery will enjoy a life of feeling the emotions of others. I have met several witches, one of which is a clan member, who can feel the emotions of animals. I have a very close friend of mine who is a shaman capable of feeling the emotions of those animals she comes into contact with. It was no great sur-prise when she went to school for equine sciences, working with horses has been a lifelong passion of hers. Another witch friend who lives just south of me is also empathic with animals, inviting every small creature imaginable into her front and back yard. Her property is loaded with bird houses and feeders to attract birds of all kinds and sizes. She reads the spirit of each animal around her, feeling their comfort and happiness because of her efforts to feed and house them. There are also those witches who receive empathic responses from plants. These may be trees, shrubs or smaller herbs. This witchery allows for the individual to connect with the plant's desires and needs.

As with all empathic abilities, when those life forms we connect with are happy, healthy and vibrant, everything is great. We feel those qualities and emotions so strongly we often reflect them in our personal lives. When those we are connected with are unhappy, sick or die, we are left feeling lost and broken. When the people we connect with shrink with age becoming sick, our empathic responses will often make us feel as if we are the ones sick and dying. It is as if we have contracted whatever illness they have through our psychic responses. Like all witcheries, empathy is a double-edged sword.

In the same way that some witches can see, and many can feel, others can hear things from the world beyond. This is often called clairaudience. Usually, this manifests as hearing spirits and will often leave the individual with this witchery feeling as if they have gone a little mad. The most common manifestation for this witchery is the hearing of a name. This may be repeated over and over at different times without warning and usually, leaves the person wondering why? This is often a spirit trying to communicate with you to gain your attention. There may be important information that it wants you to hear, or it may just want you to acknowledge its presence. There are some born with this witchery that do not hear spirits at all but rather they are able to catch glimpses of future or past conversations. One example would be a person who hears a telephone ring; a few seconds later their phone rings and they have a strange feeling come over them. This person's mind has just reached into the future slightly and picked up on the fact that someone was going to call. Even though the phone may have sounded real it was actually in the person's mind.

Along the way, I have also encountered a small number of witches that claim to smell magic and yet others who can process information through scent. However, these individuals seem to be comparatively rare, or at least when compared with other forms of witchery. One time after conversing with another practitioner through email, we decided to meet at a local restaurant. We had been talking this way for months and had never met, so it occurred to me I didn't know what he looked like. I arrived and walked into the seating area, and immediately he called out my name and waved me over to his table. I asked how he knew it was me and he stated that he could smell the magick on me.

A former coven member of ours also seemed to have an ability to receive information through scent. After some training with us in the psychic arts, I realized that she had a tendency to smell things in order to become familiar with them. During training sessions with psychometry, I realized that she was struggling to get information, so I told her to smell the object. Immediately she began to get information. For her, scent was her witchery.

During my time, I have encountered very few people, witches or otherwise, who have had a true telepathic ability. It would seem that this form of witchery is rare. I have however, encountered one truly gifted individual who was an amazingly scary telepath. She, however, was not a practicing witch. In the short time that I knew her, she seemed more than capable of reading some of the stray thoughts that those around her were thinking. She validated this for me one day, and honestly, I have to admit I was not surprised.

On a number of occasions, she seemed to be reading my mind, saying the things that I was thinking and then smiling at me knowingly. So, one day while she was distracted reading tarot cards for a client, I said to her in my head "If you can really hear what I'm thinking, set your cards down and stare at me!" Within less than a minute she did just that. She sat her cards down neatly and stared directly into my eyes. Our friendship was short lived, but her witcheries were nonetheless impressive.

I was rather surprised a few years ago, when a friend of mine, a witch from another group, blurted out "I don't have a psychic bone in my body!" I was shocked because in my training our clan devoted so much time to the development of the psychic mind. It should be noted that not all witches are necessarily "psychic" but rather that they have some limited form of witchery that allows them to process information that others cannot. Most witches are at least intuitive, with some being extremely intuitive. On the other hand, many witches are also professional psychics, embracing their natural witcheries and developing their skills so they may read accurately for others.

One form of witchery that many seem to have is the ability to project the astral body. Like all witcheries, this is a natural ability, and should not be confused with the skill that all witches are taught during their training. Those people among us who have this ability are truly blessed. Many people spend a lifetime trying to master the arts of astral projection while these individuals seem to do it on occasion as if there was nothing to it. Astral travel as a witchery seems to happen spontaneously while those gifted with it are asleep. This means that they often can't explain the experience and more often than not they have little to no control over their destination once their journey has begun.

I have met a number of witches who claim to have astral projection as their witchery, and I count myself among them. As a newborn, I had a near-death experience in the hospital. I always believed that this experience is what awakened my gift of astral projection. I remember sleeping and yet somehow walking around the house watching family members as they slept in bed or did their daily activities. At times, I would also walk around outside in my dreams watching things as they happened in the neighborhood. It always felt unbelievably real to me and was a shock when I woke up realizing that my body wasn't actually there. I have seen a number of individuals on television talk about having this ability and others like it after a near death experience or after clinically dying for a short period.

Edgar Cayce, *(March 18, 1877-January 3, 1945),* is credited as being the most documented psychic of the 20th century. Cayce is often referred to as "the Sleeping Prophet" by many because of his ability to enter a trance type state and project his astral body. Cayce did all of these things naturally with no training in the mystical arts. This is unheard of during this time period as Cayce lived prior to the "New Age Movement."

It is Edgar Cayce who is responsible for our knowledge of the Akashic records, a library filled with information pertaining to all events both past and future. Cayce would access this library using his astral body and then come back with answers and information for his clients. Cayce had many witcheries such as astral projection, prophesying, mediumship and seeing auras. He would access these abilities while in a deep trance type state. Cayce gave more than 22,362 readings in his lifetime and said;

"I am one the few who can lay aside their own personalities sufficiently to allow their souls to make the attunement to a universal source of knowledge- but I say this without any desire to brag about it. In fact, I do not claim to possess anything that other individuals do not inherently possess. Really and truly, I do not believe there is a single individual who does not possess the same ability I have. I am certain that all human beings have much greater power than they are ever conscious of- if they would only be willing to pay the price of detachment from the self-interest that it takes to develop those abilities."

Psychic dreaming or *Dreaming True*, as it is sometimes called, is another witchery that some claim to have. These dreams are usually prophetic in regards to some event that is about to happen, although some of these dreams are more symbolic as opposed to an exact re-creation. Scenarios in dreams are more abstract and sometimes more symbolic, psychic dreams are usually no different. Some individuals with this gift do not see the future but may dream of past events. It is rare to have a witch who dreams true of both the past and the future, but I am sure those individuals are out there.

Everyone's witchery manifests different, and psychic dreams are no exception. One member of our clan, a magister who ran his own coven, has the ability to hold conversations with the gods while dreaming. When he awakens, he is filled with the information that they granted him, and he must decide what, if anything to do with this knowledge. Other witches can commune with their ancestors while sleeping, while some are able to talk with the clan ancestors receiving information in regards to practicing witchcraft. This information can sometimes be used to create new rituals or learn new spells. This information is usually powerful and will wake the individual up with the strong urge to write down what they have been taught.

Throughout history, many witches have been gifted with the power of mediumship. These witches can communicate with deceased loved ones giving messages to the living. There are many psychic mediums available today who can gather information from beyond the grave. There are also many who perform channeling as a form of spirit communication as well. Some witches work with the spirits in these ways, while others perform rituals to speak with the dead, a form of necromancy.

In the biblical Book of Samuel, one can read a story about a witch with mediumistic ability. "The Witch of Endor" as she is known, was visited by King Saul to make contact with the great prophet Samuel who had died some time before. Even thou Saul was opposed to witchcraft, even enforcing the laws to repel sorcery himself, he decided to make a trip to visit this woman who was a known necromancer of her time. According to the story, the Witch of Endor was successful in conjuring the spirit of Samuel who then predicted the king's death. Looking at this story, it would seem that this witch obviously had some training in the arts, but it is unclear and undocumented if this is actually true or not. It is very likely that the Witch of Endor possessed a powerful witchery for spirit communication.

Many witches perform mediumship while in a trance type of state. This is an older practice that many covens these days have ignored out of fear. This is a form of spirit communication that is taught in our covens. We use trance work to speak with the ancestors, clan guardians, deities and the genii loci[1]. When choosing these individuals, we look for

---

1   Genius loci (pl. genii loci): guardian or protective spirit of a place

those witches who have natural witcheries in trance-working, psychic ability or who are drawn to the spirits of the dead. These individuals often make the best oracles in our clan (more on this later).

Again, if one is to look through history, there are many reports of witches not just as psychics or mediums but also as healers. These stories are often about witches using herbs, oils, ointments or charms to heal the sick. But here rather we refer to those who can heal as a natural ability. Many witches instinctively use energy to heal people. Commonly this is done by laying on hands, transferring clean, positive energy into another person to heal their mind, body or spirit.

A witch friend of ours named Stephanie heals people in this way. People always love getting healings from Steph; the energy that she channels in her healings is like nothing we have ever experienced before. We have a clan sister from one of the covens that heals people by simply talking to them. She has a knack for listening to others and then knowing just the right words or stories to tell the person in order to heal them. She is a true bard when it comes to healing through speech, and I have personally been healed in this way by her on a few separate occasions.

Magnetism or "*Occult Magnetism*" as it is sometimes called is a trained ability that some occult orders teach to their members. To understand magnetism it should be stated that I am referring to concentrated energy and not a magnetic ability as the name seems to imply. Magnetism is called such because those who use it tend to draw others to them like a moth to a flame. To accomplish this, the practitioner concentrates on drawing in energy to flood their aura, holding this energy in until it forms a brilliant cascading glow. This can be described as a small sun that surrounds the person.

As an aura reader, I have seen a few such auras. The first time was when I meant a local psychic. A friend of mine, Dave mentioned her to me, and so we decided to go pay her a visit together. We walked up the steps to her house single file and entered the front door. I turned to my right side where she was standing to greet her for the first time and was in complete shock and awe at her brilliant aura. This took me off guard to such an extreme that I could barely speak; instead, I just stared for a short time looking at the incredible golden colored energy that surrounded her entire being.

On another occasion, I was walking around in a local store shopping for some needed items. I turned to make my way down the next aisle and found a nun standing there. She turned to look at me giving me a big smile, as this happened her aura immediately grew very large and appeared to me as a beautiful rose color. I was so shocked to see this that I instantly thought I was looking at a spirit (which happens to me on occasion), only realizing that she was a physical being when she bent down to look through a box that was sitting on the bottom shelf where she stood.

Some people are able to produce this brilliant magnetic aura naturally. I personally believe that many of these people become famous in the fields of acting or politics, which some might argue are actually the same thing. Others with this naturally brilliant aura may become cult leaders. Notice that I use the word cult, not occult, which are two entirely different things. These cult leaders have a knack for draw-ing people in and then manipulating them to do what they want. These leaders are usually extremely charismatic, and those who follow them may not realize that their lives are in danger until it is too late.

This line of thought leads us to another witchery, those who have an ability to mesmerize people with their eyes and or voice. This too may be a latent talent used by some to draw others into a cult type of group. Usually, this type of witchery isn't as dramatic as most of us would like to think. Because of Hollywood and what many people call "movie magic," mesmerism tends to be thought of as a diabolical individual who encapsulates another person with mental powers and then having control of that individual, forces them through willpower to do his or her bidding.

In reality, this type of mental ability is fairly common with some people. My understanding of the art is that mesmerism has limits that make the Hollywood version almost impossible. I do have a friend however that we will call Dee. Dee is a natural with a simple technique of mesmerism. When Dee wants something or wants to sway someone's opinion on a subject, she will place her hand on them (physical contact) look them straight in the eyes and smile (gaining their trust), then speak in a soft yet commanding tone and inform them why her ideas are always correct!

Until I realized what she was doing, I had fallen victim to this little skill she had developed multiple times. I remember the look of shock on her face the first time it didn't work on me, and ever since then, I have been mindful to keep one eye on her, especially when she touches my shoulder. Dee was never trained in this art that I am aware of; it is just a natural ability that she takes advantage of when the need arises.

Some witches are reported to use what is called "*the evil*

eye." It is believed that those born under the sign of Scorpio have a natural gift with producing the evil eye. In many places, such as in Italy, the evil eye is feared by many older families. The older members of these families are often experienced in removing the evil eye using prayers and a few select components to get rid of this hex. I have seen many people with this witchery over the years (including my sister, a sun sign Scorpio) use this ability when they feel slighted by someone, even those closest to them. This will be discussed at length in chapter 3.

Another form of witchery that some witches seem able to produce naturally is the ability to control the elements. I have heard a number of witches boast about this over the years and have to admit that I thought these individuals were prone to some mental illness. However, I had had a few experiences in my time when I witnessed some of these witcheries.

When I was in my early twenties, I had been invited to a barbecue at my friend Tina's house. I'm not a huge fan of large crowds, but it was a beautiful day outside, so I decided to go. My friend who I had known for years came over to pick me up in her car; I got in, and we exchanged some hellos, then we were off to pick up a friend of hers before going to her home for the feast. Tina, who is probably the worst driver I have ever seen in my life, raced around corners while looking out her side window the whole trip there. Finally, we pulled up to her friend Pam's home, and I jumped out of the car thankful to be alive.

The two of us sat outside waiting for Pam to finish getting ready. We enjoyed the fresh air and the lovely breeze of the summer. The squirrels were playing a game of cat and mouse, chasing each other around which we assumed was for our amusement. When Pam's front door finally opened, and she stepped out to where we could see her, we immediately knew that she was in a horrible mood. The look on her face could kill, and she carried with her an aura of malice. As she walked toward us, the sun started to sink behind the clouds, and a shadow started to spread over her property. I noticed that the birds stopped singing and the squirrels were gone. As we walked to Tina's car, we both noticed that the wind picked up speed and became much colder. For a few moments, I pondered which I should be more afraid of; Tina's driving or crazy Pam?

After what seemed like a lifetime in the car with the two of them we finally arrived at the barbecue. Tina's son was cooking, and her grandchildren were running around playing in the yard. It looked to be a great day for a gathering with bright sunny skies. Tina and Pam both headed inside to finish some of the food while I stayed outside talking with some friends. Tina had set up several tables and chairs outside under the shade of a large tree, and we all sat down to eat. Finally, Pam came out of the house to join us. She sat down at our table, obviously still upset by the look on her face, not speaking a word to anyone. The other guests were pleasant and seemed to be enjoying the food. Tina's son then made the mistake of asking Pam why her boyfriend didn't come with her. Pam's reaction was to yell at him across the table, swearing like a trucker and cursing her boyfriend up and down. The guests at the table all had shocked looks on their faces as we sat there in awkward silence.

A few short moments later we heard the first crack of thunder off in the distance. Within a moment, a huge storm had gathered overhead, and everyone was grabbing stuff off the table and running indoors to escape the rain. Although

everyone including Tina seemed oblivious to it, I made
the connection that Pam was affecting the weather in her
immediate area. This seemed even more plausible when
Pam left to go home, and the rain suddenly stopped. Inter-
estingly, there were no reports of rain at all for that day, so
the fact that thunderstorms had appeared out of the blue
so quickly seemed a little suspicious to me. In combination
with the weird turn of weather, we had seen earlier outside
Pam's house that made me curious.

When I could catch Tina alone, I decided to ask her a few
questions about her friend Pam. She then told me an inter-
esting story about Pam's childhood and how she was raised
by her uncle who was heavily into the occult. Pam's parents had passed away at a young age, so her uncle adopted
her and raised her as his own. It seems that Pam had told
Tina in confidence about her upbringing, including several
rituals that she had attended as a youth. It sounded as if she
was made to attend these rituals and was not in attendance
voluntarily.

When Pam was in her mid-thirties, it seems that she had
been working full time as a psychic, channeling spirits and
such for clients out of her home; that is how Tina met her.
She was recommended by a friend of hers, and after getting her first reading with Pam, she was so impressed that
she became a regular client. Over time they grew close and
became friends. Tina also said that Pam had stopped practicing many years before I met her that day at the barbecue.
For whatever reason, it appears that Pam's channel had
ended or became blocked over time. Tina didn't have an
answer to this question, and so I didn't push the issue any
further. She did tell me however that Pam's experiences were
mostly bad and that she didn't enjoy talking about it much.

She had recently gone to a therapist because of her child-hood traumas.

A student of mine who I became very close with over the years also seems to have an affinity with electricity. While walking together in a local store, we started to have an argu-ment about something trivial; since she had already been in a mood that day after fighting with her mother on the telephone, this wasn't a big surprise. As we started to argue back and forth, I noticed that the lights in the store started to flicker. This didn't stop us from going at it and in no time, we were standing in total darkness.

I chalked that experience up to coincidence until a few weeks later when our coven had gathered in a local forest to collect material for wand crafting. My friend seemed to be in a fine mood until one of our coven mates happened to say the wrong thing, making her angry. Suddenly we had lightning overhead. Realizing that we were deep in the for-est with a thunderstorm above us was nerve racking, and we did our best to hide from the downpour. Over the next few months, I witnessed the same woman fry several electrical products after handling them for a few short moments.

 It seemed that Pam had an ability to some degree to manipulate the weather around her when she was upset. In regards to my friend, she appeared to manipulate electrici-ty specifically, again doing this when she was upset. I have seen my wife manipulate air and smoke by concentration several times. Usually, when she does this, it is small things like moving the smoke from a fire to blow in a different direction or making the wind settle down by a few degrees. One of her favorite stories involves the time she was on vacation in Fort Lauderdale. They had been on the beach for only a few minutes when a huge storm was rolling in, so she decided to push the storm away from her group by concentrating on the clouds and moving them using nothing but her mind. The clouds split in two directions going on either side of them and their hotel. She was so proud of herself that she took pictures of the storm after she had moved it.

While at a local gathering with my wife we overheard a man talking about how he could control fire. He offered a demonstration for some of those gathered near him, and being naturally nosy we decided to watch and see if he could do it. This man then made a big production of concentrating and straining his eyes, looking wild at the flames for several minutes. When nothing happened, and people begin to walk away, he suddenly became angry and left. We had a good chuckle about this man and his boasts ourselves and talked about it in the car on the way home.

It is a hard task to describe the abilities of witchery. These are latent abilities that some people possess and that others apparently do not. Sometimes, like the man who thought he could control fire with his mind, people may trick themselves into thinking that they have a witchery that they do not. For example; if a woman hears a voice in her head that says her name, should we consider this a witchery. If it happens only one or two times in a person's life, I would be inclined to say no! True witcheries tend to pop up in the individual's life over the entire course of their time on earth, perhaps even after they shed the mortal coil as well?

Perhaps this woman had a singular clairaudient experience? Perhaps she was confused? Maybe she heard her neighbor's television and thought the voices on the show were in her mind? Or, perhaps this individual needs medicine! I'm sure some witches in the modern era have been diagnosed with mental illness or perhaps have relatives who have this diagnosis. It is more than possible that witches or people with witchery from history would have been diagnosed with some form of mental delusion. But then again, we could make that argument about people from any religion or spiritual path. One does not have to have a witchery to sound a little nutty. If Christianity was not the world's leading religion, those people claiming to see fluffy winged angels floating on clouds overhead would probably be in the same category.

Why do some individuals have abilities we call witchery, while others do not? That is hard to answer in simple terms. Some athletes are naturally faster than others, while many are stronger than the average man. Some individuals will not be able to lift as much weight as many athletes can, but they may be incredibly gifted with math. Not everyone is capable of being a mathematician; some struggle to do basic math. Just because someone can do calculus in their head doesn't give them the abilities of Picasso either, painting pictures cherished by most of the world. Many scientists today are saying that these attributes are found in the person's DNA, being passed along by your direct ancestors. I couldn't agree more. I always try to express to students in our clan covens that true magick comes from within.

There are undoubtedly many forms of witchery, some of which have not been mentioned here due to space and others that are so exclusive that only a few witches seem to have that ability. There is simply not enough data on these abilities to write about them at length. Regardless of a person's witchery, their number of witcheries or the strength of those abilities, if an individual displays one of these natural powers they are showing a potential for witchcraft.

2

Blood of the Red Rose

The power is in the blood! As witches, we believe that the power comes from the blood and that this power can be passed down to future generations in what we call, "*The Red Thread*". This thread is symbolic of the witch's bloodline, but it is also more than symbolic as it connects the witch to the ancestry of his or her people. Some believe that this thread is passed down only from mother to daughter, that it is the female side of the family that carries the genes of witchery. Personally, I don't believe that this is true. Both man and woman seem more than capable of passing on witch blood to the next generation of their families.

Essentially this is DNA, or more appropriately, the magick code in your DNA that carries your power. Witch blood is an encoded memory that sings as it flows through your body. The ancestors will speak to you through your witch blood if you let them. The voices of your ancestors are hidden beneath your flesh, flowing through your veins; here they are still alive with the spark of magick ready to speak to those who will listen.

The true power of witchcraft comes from the witch's blood, and some witches seem to have more "blood power" than others. This may simply be due to the witch's ancestry, power being passed down from generation to generation through the blood. Sometimes this may skip a generation and then appear again stronger with the following generation. However, most do not recognize it or ever attempt to use it. It will often manifest naturally and spontaneously as a form of witchery.

Another way that one may acquire witch blood is through reincarnation. The term reincarnation is used lightly here, and should not be confused with the Hindu belief in reincarnation. (I would suggest looking into works concerning "Fate vs. Reincarnation" by others who follow today's craft, of which there are many to choose.) Living a life or many lives in previous incarnations as a practicing witch could undoubtedly leave some memories of spell crafting, wort-cunning or possibly the initiation process. When that person springs forth from the cauldron of souls, he or she may be able to instinctually use some of that previous knowledge as time goes on. Spirit can saturate the blood with memory, however making use of it is another story altogether.

Many practitioners of today's traditional witchcraft claim that witch blood originated from Azazel. The basic idea behind this first appeared in Paul Huson's classic book; *Mastering Witchcraft, a Practical Guide for Witches, Warlocks and Covens*- first printed in 1970 by G.P. Putnam's Sons. Since that time there have been many witches, covens, and clans that have done incredible research into this claim.

Azazel is one name for the god of witchcraft among today's witches. It is believed that he and the other angelic beings of his order choose to mate with the children of the earth, thus producing a new race that was gifted with supernatural powers. This new race referred to as the Nephilim, were described as giants from various sources. For many modern witches, credit is given to Azazel and the Watchers for teaching witchcraft as well as the mystical arts, sciences and warfare to our ancient ancestors. It is of the blood of the Watchers and the Nephilim that many believe the source of witchcraft on earth has derived.

From the Sethite point of view, the Nephilim descended from Seth, the son of Adam. Thus, we find the reference to the Nephilim as the "*Sons of God.*" In this belief, the Nephilim are not the children of angelic beings, but rather they have sprung from the loins of holy men who descended from the first man himself, Adam. Today's witches reject this theory, working with Azazel who has many names among the craft, sighting the reference to the "*Sons of God*" to be a term used for angels and their choirs.

The most common thought regarding the Nephilim remains that they are the descendants of the Watchers, angels sent to earth to watch over humanity. It is believed that these Watchers were asked to reside on earth with the people of that time in order to guide them. The Watchers followed their orders, descending to earth where it is believed that they became tangible. What the Watchers did not realize is that they would be stuck on earth unable to return to the heavens. Because of this, many people have categorized the Watchers as fallen angels. Indeed, the word Nephilim seems to derive from the Hebrew word *naphal* meaning "*to fall.*"

Another possible source for witch blood comes to us from the Celtic lands, primarily from Ireland and Wales and can be found in the stories of the *Tuatha de Dannon*, "*the Children (or Tribes) of Danu*." An earlier name for these people seems to be *Tuath De*, meaning "*Tribe of Gods*." Like the Nephilim previously mentioned, the Tuatha were believed to have supernatural powers unseen by the Celtic people until the time of their arrival. Also, like the Nephilim, the Tuatha were said to have taught the people of Ireland many skills including magick, science, agriculture, blacksmithing, and weaponry.

Eventually, the Tuatha were defeated and driven from the Celtic lands. However, there are many recorded stories of the Tuatha reappearing much later in history. This seems to indicate that these supernatural beings were immortal and at some point, the Celtic peoples began to worship them as gods. Although some writings depict the Tuatha as heroes, kings, queens or fey, their status as gods has many parallels with pantheons from other cultures. Is it possible that these supernatural beings, the Tuatha, were actually Watchers of the angelic order? Could the Tuatha be the Nephilim that survived the flood in the time of Noah coming to the shores of Europe? It is said that the Tuatha arrived on ships or boats and that the Celtic people knew that they were not of this world. Among the Celtic Tuatha, we find giants such as the Dagda and Bran who later became gods. We also find multiple stories of fey creatures the Celts called the *sidhe*. Some of these Sidhe beings were also said to be giant in size.

Like many other mythologies of the time, the Tuatha were believed to have mated with humans producing what the ancients called demigods. Some of these demigods like Cu Chulainn, son of Lugh, are similar to demigods found in Greek and Roman myths. Achilles was said to be born of a mortal man and a nymph goddess, Agenor was the son of Poseidon, while Perseus was the son of Zeus by a mortal woman. Like the story of the Watchers who produced the Nephilim, the Pagan stories of old seem to have the same concept of higher beings that mated with us mere mortals causing the bloodline to produce children with extraordinary abilities. These demigods of old like their angelic or godly parents would be most likely to follow suit, mating with humans spreading the seeds of divinity to produced new generations of supernatural beings. Although the following generations may be a much watered-down version of the original demigods, they would, however, carry within them a power in their blood.

In her book, The Rebirth of Witchcraft Pg. 83-84, Doreen Valiente, writes:

> "In the Channel Islands of Jersey, where there were many witch trials, it is said that down to comparatively modern days some families secretly pride themselves on being of 'le grand sang'- that is having witches blood in their veins."

In French, *Le Grand Sang* means *"the Large Blood"* and is probably used here as a way of acknowledging the witches' supernatural abilities as being large or perhaps larger than life in the eyes of the common folk. The *Sangreal Sodality*, formed by William G. Gray and Jacobus G. Swart was founded in November of 1980 and has since established temples of its brotherhood in North America, Brittan, and South Africa. The Sangreal Sodality is a magical order that teaches its followers about the power within the blood. The word *sangreal* is used to mean *"royal blood"* or *"authentic blood"* by the group's members who believe that they can awaken the divine spark inside of themselves through the use of magick.

Regardless of its origins, witch blood will burn like fire when it is used properly in magick; because of this we often call it *Ignem Serpentes*. Using the power of your witch blood for magical purposes will most likely leave you feeling drained, depressed or possibly sick for some time after. You are essentially depleting your own energy supply and will need to recharge it in some way. We teach those members of our clan to draw energy from various sources when performing magick with their witch blood; however, there will be times when this is not possible due to the operation, or because of the situation, you may find yourself in.

Another term used by witches, *The White Thread*, refers to blood ties that are symbolic at the initiation. The white thread represents an adoption, for lack of a better term, into the coven as an initiated member. Although this is not physical (such as the red thread discussed above), it is a magickal adoption, meaning that you are now a part of our family.

This adoption is what makes up most of today's hereditary craft. If one looks down their own family tree, they may find a relative that had practiced witchcraft, divination or sorcery. It's possible that they may find that they have several. Investigating this may, on the other hand, turn up no documented evidence of witch blood, but before there was the written language, there was Pagan magick. Everyone in the world today has Pagan ancestors, even if it's not documented someplace.

Once a witch makes their pact with the covenant, and they are given the blood oath, they are family and will always be family. True family has little to do with blood. True families are those people or groups of people that you treat like family. In turn, if they are true family, they will treat you the same. The *Blood Oath of the Clan* is forever. The oath has the power to change your thread, binding the clan ancestry to you, while in turn binding you to the ancestors. If the oath of a witch's covenant is broken, that witch has cursed themselves, and they alone must face the ancestors for this heresy.

Clan members who are family are given the witch's mark at initiation. This may be done differently in other clans or family traditions, but regardless of the process or placement, the mark links you to the clan as a family member. The blood oath and the witch's mark are traditionally given with the red knife. The word red here is in reference to blood, but also to the handle of the tool itself which is often stained red and decorated with symbols of the witch's god.

The red knife is sometimes called a *shelg* or *sacrificial blade*. Other times simply referred to as the *Secret Tool of the Crafter*. This tool is commonly used by some witches for blood magick, meaning bloodletting as a component in spell casting. Shelgs were originally used for making a small cut for this purpose as well as during the oath taking. When the shelg is used for blood magick, it has a way of empowering the components of the spell, but may also bind components together. This may be done purposefully or accidently if the witch is not careful.

Some witches use the red knife in necromancy rituals; a process our clan members call "feeding" the spirits or making a "red offering" to the ancestors. If the working is to be a red offering, the witch should have a specially kept bowl for this purpose. This offering is always given freely of the witch seeking to work with the dead from the finger of Venus or the finger of Saturn depending on the work to be performed. Some people who read this may take it as evidence that witches perform animal sacrifice. I have never met a witch who did this type of working. Like all things of the past, this may or may not have been the way of our ancestors. It is also possible that there are some solitary practitioners out there who do this type of red offering today. I cannot say one way or the other.

Calling the shelg a knife could be a little misleading when being read by some. Most shelgs are shaped more like an awl or thick needle as opposed to a sharp blade. Shelgs are not used for actual cutting; it is more of a poke than anything else. Many witches these days don't use the shelg at all anymore, preferring to use a sterile medical lancet for the blood oath. However, the shelg should be present at initiations for symbolic reasons as well as for the obvious magickal ones.

Blood magick is performed in many ways. This may be done in conjunction with candle magick by smearing one's witch blood onto the candle similar to an anointing. The witch may also drip his or her blood onto the candle while chanting or invoking. Of course, these are only a few examples of how a witch may use blood for spell work. Blood as a component can be used to empower many spells, but one must take great heed in the chosen operation and purpose of the spell. It is truly not wise to use your blood for all spell casting. Knowing when it is appropriate and when it is inappropriate are lessons that all clan members must learn. One thing we teach our members is that blood can be used by the witch to bind their energy to some of the tools of the craft. In doing this, the witches spirit touches the spirit of the tool making the magickal link between them much stronger.

Sometimes, witches in our clan will use what we call the *Blood of the Red Lion or Blood of the Red Moon.*

The *Blood of the Red Lion* is blood taken from a magister, while the *Blood of the Red Moon* is that taken from a magistra. This is usually, but not always, taken from one of the five fingers specifically chosen for its magical attributes. An herbal substitute for a witch's blood is often dragons blood resin. One of the attributes of dragon's blood is that it adds power to that which it touches. Mixing this component with other ingredients in recipes gives them a boost, similar to the witch's blood but not as potent as the real thing. The creation of sigils is often done with dragon's blood or real blood added to the ink when appropriate.

To truly understand how this substitution is possible one only needs to understand the basic ideas of sympathetic magic and the magical correspondence of components used in spell craft. Sympathetic magick makes up most of today's modern witchcraft as a form of low magick or earth magick. Today, witches employ sympathetic magic for almost every spell they cast. Sympathetic magick, also known as imitative magick, is a practice based on imitation or correspondence.

One of the most common forms of imitation magick found today is the use of poppets. Many people today know them only as voodoo dolls. These are little dolls formed to look like the crude image of a specific person they intend to target with magick. In witchcraft, we call these poppets. We use these in magick to represent the person the spell is being cast on. Thus it imitates the person's image and through concentration and magickal operation what we do to one influences the other.

Magickal correspondence is based on the idea that objects

may influence each other based on their similarities or resemblance. Ancient beliefs, such as those found in the *Doctrine of Signatures* [2], regard the properties of plants used in folk medicine to be sympathetic in nature. For example; the Doctrine of Signatures states that "red beet juice is good for the blood." Why did people believe this? Because they are both red and so they must be akin to each other. There are hundreds of such examples found in many books giving medicinal advice (much of which could be deadly) based on the idea of imitation or sympathetic correspondence. This is the same basic idea that witches use when performing sympathetic magick.

In his classic book on mythology and comparative religion, *The Golden Bough* [3], Sir James George Frazer gives the following as an example of sympathetic and contagious magics.

> "Law of Contact or Contagion may be called Contagious Magic. Contagious magic commits that assuming that things which have once been in contact with each other are always in contact. But in practice, the two branches are often combined. "

When we use blood or other bodily fluids in magick, we could categorize this as contagious magick. However, when we witches do this, we simply call it a psychic link. That is an object of the person's which holds within it, their personal energy by means of contact or contagion. This is most often done by acquiring something of your target; an article of clothing, a piece of jewelry, nail clippings, a lock of hair or a small amount of bodily fluid (if possible). This links

---

2   The Doctrine of Signatures, dating from ancient Greece, is the belief that certain plants can be used to treat ailments in those body parts that they resemble.

3   First published in 1890

your spell to the target, essentially guiding your magick where you want it to go.

Simply put, sympathetic/contagious magick plus energy channeled in various forms such as- dancing, chanting, drumming and praying with emotion, will often lead to the materialization of the witch's desires. A witch who uses their own blood in magick is adding their power or influence over a person, object or situation. Applying the witch's blood to another person's poppet is only done to gain control over that individual or to influence them greatly by will power.

Other types of blood or fluid used in magick such as the *Blood of the Red Dragon* or *Blood of the Red Rose* is only used for specific types of magick. *Blood of the Red Dragon* is not actually blood at all, but rather is the ejaculate of a male witch. This, being part of the male mysteries of the craft, is both literal and symbolic.

Just as the *Blood of the Red Dragon* is dualistic in its meaning, symbolism, and mysticism, so too is the *Blood of the Red Rose*.

Blood of the Red Rose can be either vaginal fluids or menstrual blood from a female witch. When used as a component in specific types of magick, the *Blood of the Rose* is raw, transformative energy. The rose is often symbolic of the Yoni or reproductive power of the Divine Goddess. Its symbolism is the sacred power of the feminine mystery, the procession of ancestry and the blossoming of new life on the thread of fate. In the *Blood of the Red Rose* we find initiation into the mystical realm of the Blood Mother. Here we do not just find the thread of life, but that of death as well. For as the rose grows blossoms and becomes exalted, it will in time begin to fade, decay and transform into the next stage of its fate.

In the *Blood of the Red Rose*, we also find the mystical and symbolic meaning of the term *Sub Rosa*, or "*Under the Rose of Secrecy.*" The rose, with its sharp thorns and beautiful petals has long been a symbol of confidentiality and initiation into secret mysteries of witchcraft. Meetings or rituals held in secrecy often make use of the rose; this can be either literal or by use of symbolic imagery. Sub Rosa used in this way denotes the blood oath of the craft. It's bloody thorns begin to drip the moment an initiate speaks the words. When those words are completed, he or she is then bound by oath under the rose.

It is certainly no secret among today's occultists that the rose has long been associated with the pentagram. We will not discuss the history of the pentagram here, but rather its association with the rose specifically due to the space allowed in this work. While there are many types of roses found today, including the four-petaled rose, sometimes referred to as the Celtic rose, it is the five-petaled rose that is mentioned here as a symbol synonymous with the pentagram. While the pentagram is recognized as a masculine symbol by most, by examination of the rose, we begin to find the feminine associations of this symbol as well.

To the Greek philosopher, Pythagoras, the pentacle, because of its five points, was the number and symbol of the human experience. Because the Greeks divided the human body and the soul into five parts, the pentagram or PentAlpha was representative of the five elements: Earth, Air, Fire, Water, and Psyche. Thus, these elements were seen in the human form with its arms extended out and the legs spread apart. The fifth element of Psyche was found in the head which was held upright. The Babylonians had discovered that the path of the planet Venus could be found by tracing the pattern of the five-pointed star and used the symbol in the worship of Ishtar. Later the Greeks and Romans used it as symbols for their goddesses, Venus and Aphrodite, respectively.

Among the Greek myths, we find a story of the rose as a magickal symbol having sexual connotations as well as those of secrecy. The rose was used by the goddess Aphrodite to keep her indiscretions hidden. To do this Aphrodite presented a rose to her son Eros, the Greek god of love. Eros, in turn, presented that rose to Harpocrates, the god of silence so that her affairs may stay secret. Thus, the rose and the pentagram became symbols of Aphrodite (via Venus, via Ishtar), sexuality and secrets kept by means of silence.

Rosicrucian orders also use the rose as a magickal symbol and can be found in The Rose Cross. The image of the rose cross is widely used today and has many interpretations by different practitioners and magickal groups who focus on the symbolism found within its imagery. In the Middle Ages, it was common to have a rose suspended over a council table or hung from the entrance point of a room; those entering the chamber would swear an oath of secrecy to keep those things discussed in silence.

When our clan leaders meet for council, we place a large cauldron in the center of the room, if the meeting is to take place outdoors we will create a fire in the cauldron to burn as a source of inspiration and creative willpower. The members sit in a circle around this cauldron which becomes the *axis mundi* of the meeting place. A rose is passed along the circle from member to member, each repeating the blood oath of the clan.

The oath of secrecy is vital for witchcraft and those that practice its mysteries should always be sub-rosa. In my time, I have known a few witches who have betrayed the blood oath. Some of these witches followed different traditions or paths, but all paid the price of the Blood Mother for breaking the sacred promise.

3

Anointed Eyes

With the newly anointed eyes of initiation, the witch begins to instinctually understand their craft better. The process involved leads one to the discovery of what we call the *Eyes of Spirit*. This is, in fact, one in a trinity of attributes received by the initiated. In our clan, we call these three gifts the *Voice of the Dragon*, the *Eyes of Spirit* and the *Ear of the Gods*. With anointed eyes, we begin to see with the eyes of spirit. This should not be taken as a literal translation; you do not become a master clairvoyant overnight simply because you have been anointed as part of an elevation. If you are properly trained, and effort is put forth, this will enhance that which the initiate has already gained during the first and second degrees of training.

With *Eyes of Spirit*, the witch becomes a channel allowing the gods and ancestors to look through their eyes. Sometimes they will guide you this way; this may happen in many ways. Sometimes they may show you the intentions others unveiling truths that can lie hidden behind people' words. The *Eyes of Spirit* will help you to see the mysteries of magick and learn the ways of the ancestors.

Most witches are trained in the psychic arts, developing those skills with which they are naturally inclined towards. Hopefully, they will learn a few new skills with some degree of proficiency. The *Eyes of Spirit* may enhance these abilities, but that also depends upon the witch and their degree of effort. When we perform trance work, channeling and other psychic powers on the mystical pathway, we strengthen the connection with the world of phantasm. By the time the witch has completed the training process, this otherworldly presence should be very strong, upon the final initiation, this presence never truly leaves.

It is said that you can tell the strength of a witch by his or her eyes! It is this strength which is the secret to utilizing the powers of the witch's eye, a process that some seem to have a natural affinity for, while others will spend many months trying to develop the abilities of this art.

As practitioners of magick, witches understand the power of energy manipulation.

Magick is Energy- Energy is Magick!

With this basic concept of magick, it is easy to see the different ways that witches can direct the flow of energy with their hands, fingers, and eyes. Once this is understood- any spell can be transferred via the witch's eye. Just like the witch is trained at the first degree to charge objects with their hands, a witch is also trained to use the witch's eye to charge objects. A trained witch may use the power of their eyes to charge sigils, crystals, candles and more. They may also learn the art of fascination. Most often this is accomplished by use of a mirror or a fascination ring/stone.

You will need to use all of your emotions and possibly the power of your voice or hand gestures as an aid in this process. When done correctly, the person is surrounded with your emotions and drawn in with your eyes. To overthrow another person, draw up power (energy) from your center and then project it through your eyes, if possible straight at the person's third eye, pushing hard your thoughts and emotions. It is believed by many witches that their eyes can pierce the veil between the worlds and that this can be used for divination as well as to cast spells. When you master the skill of the witch's eye, you will find it possible to use a photograph of your intended target getting the same results.

There are many stories of witches, much of which comes from Italy, talking about the *evil eye*. This is an ability used by witches to deliver curses by transference of energy through the eyes. It is believed that this is performed by a witch who is jealous of the victim and so he or she projects this jealousy out of their eyes cursing the person with the evil eye.

In the Italian language, the evil eye is known as the *malocchio*. In Sicily, however, it is called *jettatore*. A few years ago, I had a coworker named Dominic whose family had come directly from Italy. His mother who was from Sicily told me of the jettatore and how she was taught to get rid of the curse. In a boiling pot of water, she would add several drops of olive oil. She would then stir the oil into the water while praying vigorously a series of Catholic prayers. The cursed person was then anointed on the forehead while more prayers were recited. This could go on for some time, ending when she felt the curse was gone. A friend of mine

Kathleen used to wear a series of small gold charms around her neck all the time. When I asked her about these, she told me that they were given to her by her grandmother to protect her from the evil eye. One of these small charms looks like the horn of Italy but is called the *cornicello*, meaning "*little horn*." This cornicello is a twisted horn-shaped amulet. The other was in the shape of a hand with index and pinky finger pointing down toward the ground. This gesture is often called the *mano cornuta*, or the "*sign of the horns*".

In Spain, *mal de ojo* is the name given for the evil eye, while in Turkey it is sometimes called the *nazar*. The name for the "*envious eye*" in Hebrew is *Ayin ha'ra*. In Jewish culture, the *hamsa*, sometimes known as the "*Hand of Miriam*" is worn as a protective amulet. This charm is shaped like a hand with the fingers pressed together as if to say, "Stop!" or "Halt!" The word hamsa means five, perhaps referring to the five fingers on the hand. Some of these hamsa charms are made to be very stylish with any number of designs carved into the center of the hand. Some hamsa talismans are created with a blue eye in the center of the hand's palm.

The evil eye has been reported to cause harm to children as well as adults, livestock, pets and crops simply by walking past them and casting an envious gaze.

It should be noted that the witch's eye can be used for many types of magick, the evil eye only being one such example of its potential. The witch's eye is just as likely to be used for healing, protection, or to seduce someone as much as it is for cursing. Of course, history tends to record the negative actions of people more so than the beneficial, and this seems to be doubly true of anything involving the word "witch".

The psychic and magickal strength of the witch is shown through the windows of the eyes. It is important that you be able to cast this power from the eyes with the greatest of concentration. This energy is being transferred into ritual objects or spell components such as cords, candles, and poppets. When the witch has developed this skill, he or she may send thoughts through their eyes.

To develop the witch's eye, long hours will be spent standing before a mirror staring into one's own eyes developing the proper gaze and building the required exchange of energy. This is actually a loop of energy, a type of Mobius built up by concentration and technique. Of course, the witch may use a crystal ball, brass bowl, or a cauldron filled three-thirds of the way with water. Black mirrors, used for scry-ing, are not the best choice for developing the witches gaze. The image needs to be clear and well-lit to get the proper stare.

Start with five-minute increments and increase the length of time after a few days. Stand before the mirror with your eyes closed at first and concentrate upon your desire. Do this until your psychic mind is flooded with raw potential and emotion. Now open your eyes and gaze into the mir-ror concentrating on the Mobius of energy, its flow, and ebb, letting it grow strong by focus. When you feel that the power has built to the proper level, take your gaze from the reflective surface and try to transfer this built-up energy by charging an object selected ahead of time.

This should give the beginner enough to start with. In regards to building upon the technique, the witch is only limited by their own imagination. The use of such magick has great potential.

4

Ignem Serpentes

The serpernt and the dragon are often synonymous with
each other in mythology. These two creatures symbol-
ize life, creation, regeneration, death, destruction, fertility,
wisdom and healing to name but a few. Serpent and dragon
myths can be found in every corner of the ancient world.
The word Serpent derives from the Latin *serpens* which
means snake or, an animal that crawls. In our clan, we use
the energy of the serpent for expressing our willpower in a
technique we call the *"Voice of the Dragon"* (or Serpent). To
understand this technique a little better we must first discuss the power of the spoken word as used by the ancients.

When we speak of the *Voces Magicae* in the clan; we are
referring to ancient languages, symbols, and writings that
are used as words of power in a ritual format. The *Voces
Magicae* can be traced back to ancient texts regarding
the power of the spoken word. In ancient Egypt when
words were spoken or written, they were believed to have
special powers contained within them. Many people see
hieroglyphs for example and believe them to be pictures

conveying information. What most do not realize is that the words and symbols of the Egyptians contained within them realities that lent to their power. Many words of power spoken in the Egyptian tongue do not have the same magical effect when spoken in another language. English, for example, does not contain the same sequence of letters when put together and vocalized.

Another source referencing the voces magicae appears in tomes from ancient Greece. In the 4th century BCE, we find the Greek book "Ephesia Grammata," a magical text that references the *Voces Magicae* as words of power. The text describes three branches of magick as follows; Goetia (low magick), Mageia (general magick) and Theourgia (high magick).

If we look at the *Voces Magicae* used in Theourgia as a way of identifying with divinity, we can see how it lends to the soul's transformational abilities. Through the use of Theourgia, one may be touched by divinity and thus becomes cleansed. By expanding on the basic ideas of the voces magicae, one can begin to see how the witch can use these words of power in order to accomplish many goals. This may be considered a form of Goetia, depending upon the spell or ritual itself. However, it does not always fit into such a neat little box as such a simple description may seem to apply.

When used the magickal operation, the *Voces Magicae* is meant to be used by the witch to speak spontaneously as opposed to reading from a scripted set of invocations. The focus needed for ritual invocation is hard to achieve when reading from a piece of parchment. These words are to be spoken with much passion and conviction to be done properly. When performed correctly the *Voces Magicae* is said to call forth spirits who are usually protective in nature.

I have been witness to a few practitioners of the arts that have successfully used the voce magicae during ritual while reading from a paper or book; however, these were experienced witches and magicians who have mastered the *Voice of the Dragon*.

The voces magicae is one way that our clan members make use of the *Voice of the Dragon*. This is the *Voces Magicae* used by an initiate to speak words of power to cause great change such as summoning or banishing a spiritual force. The words spoken are often in Latin, Greek or Egyptian. The use of other languages such as French, Italian or English do not carry the same vibration as those I have mentioned. However, they can still pack a punch if the practitioner is proficient with the technique.

The *Voice of the Dragon* is one of the three gifts gained by the initiate. With the power of the gods rushing through the psychic channels, the witch priest is embraced by the ancestors of old. It's now up to him or her to allow the Gods to speak through their voice. The witch in the role of priest or priestess is the earthly representation of the gods, a manifestation that allows the voice of the spirits to be heard by the ears of man and spirit alike. With the *Voice of the Dragon* one may speak soft and gentle words to heal the sick or speak thunderous words to drive away the profane inhabitants found in the world of phantasm.

When learning to use the power of one's voice many hours are spent chanting and vibrating. The words of power found in the magickal texts regarding the *Voces Magicae* are considered untranslatable by scholars. Most of these words appear to be created by using a long series of vowels strung together as the base. The technique that many magicians practice today in order to learn proper vibration used for invocation looks like this; A-A-A-A-A-A-A- E-E-E-E-E-E-E- I-I-I-I-I-I-I-O-O-O-O-O-O-O -U-U-U-U-U-U-U. Thus, simulating some of the sounds found in these ancient texts.

Invocations are often vibrated loudly so that all present feel the energy rushing through them like a wave of power. Invocation (as opposed to the evocation) is used to call a power from within to be present in a ritual. Aleister Crowley writes in, Magick in Theory and Practice[4], Chapter XV:

> "The whole secret may be summarized in these four words: Enflame thyself in praying."

This is sound advice for anyone who is on the path of using the *Voces Magicae*. Invocation should spew from the mouth of the dragon engulfing those in your ring until the ritual is lifted up by the power called. It is easy to get lost inside of the self during the ecstasy of invocation. When done right, an invocation can be a euphoric experience.

By using the *Voice of the Dragon* as mentioned above, the words of power are channeled from the solar plexus and then expelled through the mouth. This leads us to another way that witches in our clan are trained to use the dragon energy. By absorbing the *Ignem Serpentes* (or *Ignem Dracones*), large amounts of energy gather in the stomach area where it is felt the strongest; this becomes the seat where the dragon rests.

The soul has long been associated with the solar plexus leading to the euphemism, "the seat of the soul" which is often in reference to the stomach or solar plexus region of the human body. By tapping into the "*Ignis Terra Deorsum*",

4   Magick in Theory and Practice by Aleister Crowley first published in 1924

or, *"Fire below the Earth"*, and mixing it with the witch's power that has accumulated in the seat of the soul, the witch can accomplish many magickal feats without depleting their personal energies. My close friend and fellow magister, Orius, was taught to call the earth's fire, *"Sarf Ruth"*, a Cornish term meaning *"Fire in the Land."*

There are numerous references in Celtic legend to dragons that appear at times either with wings or without (serpents). These great beasts were believed to dwell in the landscape, found in such places as caves or deep underground. The Druids, who were connected to these ancient beings seemed capable of tracking the movement of the dragons who traveled beneath the earth. Today we call these ley lines. The Celtic people seem to have understood the power of these dragon paths and may have been instructed by the Druids to build settlements or monuments along some of these ley lines.

The *Fire below the Earth* (or *Fire in the Land* if you prefer) is visualized as a great serpent (or dragon) whose body is made of flames and slithers like lava. These ancient beings are often called the *Ignem Serpentes*, or *"Serpents Fire"* which is rooted in the earth's magma core and spreads out underground becoming ley lines where its energy accumulates in sacred places.

The witch only needs to concentrate on the *Ignem Serpentes* to tap into its energy. By adding the appropriate visualization and enough force, the energy will respond and follow your thoughts. Many witches will use a stang or staff to connect with this great serpent, tapping into ley lines pulling its energy up to the surface where it is then shaped and directed. One use of this technique is to cast a circle about the working space, a circle of fire or *Circulum Ignis;* we cast with the staff or stang. This can also be referred to as the *Baculum Medio Ardentis Flammae*, the staff (or stang) of burning flames.

It is usually best if the witch practices with the *Serpents Fire* outdoors, at least in the beginning. If you have a fire pit or space where you hold regular ritual fires, this is the perfect location to tap into the serpent's energy. Constant use of the same sacred space creates a type of portal into another realm. In this case, that portal leads into and out of a realm where fire and earth have combined. Drawing up the Ignem Serpentes here should feel natural and allow for easier contact since it is already a receptacle of fire energy.

To begin any technique using the *Serpents Fire* you should use your basic relaxation method until your body is limp and your mind is relaxed. With this accomplished, you should now put your psychic focus on the earth's core. With concentration, visualize a glowing red serpent slowly rising up from the magma deep within the earth. See this snake extending its body, slithering through the soil and the rock.

As its body elongates, it gets closer and closer to you. Feel the serpent beneath you. When this snake emerges from the ground, see it attach itself to you or your stang like an umbilical cord. Let the *Ignem Serpentes* fill you with energy. Feel this energy merging with your blood, burning with power and light.

Focusing on your solar plexus (it is here that the dragon rests), allow the energy to grow. After a few moments, concentrate on the energy spreading out moving through your veins. At this point, you have several options:

1) **Create the Circulum Ignis** -Begin to move the fire up

your torso pushing it towards your arms and down to your hands. With your staff or stang, you can now channel the *Circulum Ignis* about your working space. Concentrate on pushing the fire out and away from you while forming it with your will power.

2) *Energy Transference and Mirror Magick* -Begin to move the fire up your torso pushing it towards your arm and down your power hand. Shape the fingers of your power hand into a triangle of force using the fingers of Venus, Jupiter, and Saturn. Now, direct the serpent's fire out of your fingers in the shape of a bolt or dart. This technique works well with mirror magick, using the mirror as a portal to deliver your energy. This should not be confused with the witch's black mirror which is used for divination. Mirror magick is a technique that many witches use to deliver certain spells.

3) *Dragons Breath* -With this exercise, you will be mixing the serpents fire with your breath. The lungs are capable of holding seven pints of air, even though we use far less on average. Begin to move the fire up your torso into your lungs. Keeping the mouth closed breathe only through the nostrils. Continue breathing this way letting the fire gather here until you have filled your lungs to their full capacity. To do this, feel the fire expanding in your cavity growing like a balloon as you inhale. When you feel that the fire in your lungs has peaked, open your mouth and begin to breathe out the fire. Push the energy out each time you exhale until you have filled your surroundings with serpent's fire. Your immediate area should feel energized.

ᔐ

Controlling the breath is key to mastering some magickal tecŠiques including trance work and energy manipulation. Breathing rapidly to excite the heart and the mind is another way to manipulate and expel one's personal energy. Performing this type of rapid breath control allows one to push their energy further and may be used in combination with other magickal formulas. Pulling breath up from the solar plexus and breathing on an object is a way to empower that item, often referred to as giving it the *"breath of life"*. Giving breath is also a common practice in Hoodoo magick when empowering a mojo hand or gris-gris bag.

Coven members often employ synchronized breathing techniques when working together. The unison of this practice creates a rhythm which then leads to an altered state of consciousness. Breathing in a rhythmic pattern is one way to control the breath as well as one's heart rate. There are different patterns of breathing that the practitioner may employ such as counting the breath in and counting the same number out. An example would be for the coven to gather in a circle with all members facing in towards the center. A pattern of four breaths is chosen, which goes like this; inhaling through the nostrils to the count of 1-2-3-4, exhaling out the mouth to the count of 1-2-3-4. This is repeated over and over in an unbroken chain. Usually, a coven leader will help to keep the group focused by raising the wand up for inhaling and lowering the wand while exhaling.

The breath control method as mentioned above produces a large amount of raw energy that the coven may use for mental sorcery, healing, or to empower an artifice with vital energy before sending it on its merry way to complete a task. The coven may also combine these breathing techniques with those of the Ignem Serpentes, exhaling the serpent's fire out in unison to consecrate a charm or empower a magickal device.

5

Betwixt and Between

In the hours of twilight set between the sun and the moon, we find the true sabbatic rituals of the witch's craft. It is in this twilight place of the mind that the door shall open and the processions of spirits gather to march across the land in rhythm with the season. In this time, by means of their unguent, the witch may fly the fairy paths within the secret world of spirit. It is here that the gods and fey creatures are both real and archetypes. They are both alive, and yet they are not alive. For when we are betwixt the worlds in the witch's ring, we find that in the sabbat rituals there is paradox around every corner.

Witches of the world have always sought out the intermediate places in nature to gather and perform their sabbat rites. In these places, we are neither wholly in one place or another. We can step betwixt the world in certain places where the landscape is met by two or more elements, luminaries or other natural phenomena. It is in these places that the witch can catch glimpses into the fey realm and communicate with the ancestors. Places such as seashores, where water and earth have formed a meeting place; where the boundary between two great powers is present but not completely stable nor permanent. Caves, volcanoes, and misty meadows are other such places where we might step between the worlds for a time, for these places themselves are betwixt.

The same can be said of some animals as well. By their nature toads heave an ability to enter into the secret world. The toad can traverse between land and water, the physical world and the spiritual world. As a totemic creature, toads and frogs teach the witch the arts of spirit walking and metamorphosis. The toad as a creature that is half in this world and half in the next world teaches the witch to keep one eye in the spirit world at all times. Toads and frogs are often witches familiars for this reason, and the witch who works with the toad is learning the lessons of personal power and how to use that power. Many charms and devices can be made with toad bones and skin; some of these charms include protection, healing, astral projection, and weather working. It is believed by witches that when the toad croaks, it's calling the rains to fall upon the land.

Other creatures that have the ability to traverse betwixt the worlds are the cat, the crow, the owl and the horse. The cat whose brain is always in a state of alpha has the ability to pierce the veil between the worlds and see things in the hidden realm that many people cannot. Because the cat's psychic mind is always active in this way, its perception denotes it as otherworldly. Like toads and hares, the cat is often a witch's familiar. Associated with the moon, the cat represents both magick and mystery in the physical and spiritual world. The cat familiar teaches the witch to be independent and to trust one's instincts.

The crow, as a totemic animal has many gifts and is revered in many cultures as a creature of the underworld who is associated with many deities of that realm. Crows often deliver messages for the ancestors, the fey and the gods in the lower realm. Witches often use crows and ravens to send messages to the Dark Goddess. The crow is revered for its intellect and its secret ability to speak with witches through omens of prophecy.

The horse is a true walker between the worlds. As a totemic creature, the horse is known for its ability to ride the witch on its back through the astral realm by jumping the hedge and acting as a guide into the underworld. The witch who finds themselves akin to the horse spirit is learning the lessons of freedom by means of travel and may experience many journeys betwixt the worlds. In some European lands witches were said to ride on the back of black goats to the sabbatic ritual, an obvious totem of the Horned God, the goat is renowned for its ability to overcome obstacles, even those they encounter while traversing the astral world.

In our clan, we believe as the ancient Celts did, that certain places in nature are sacred. The Druids called these wild lands, Nemetons. You can find the root word, *nemet*, as the prefix in Nemeton, being used to describe various locations from Scotland to Turkey. In Germanic history, we find the Nemete tribe who occupied the region once known as Palatinate. The people of the Nemete worshiped a goddess who they called Nemetona. These Nemetons were used by the Celtic people who gathered among groves of trees as well as other places in nature where the landscape was natural and filled with ancestral memory. The covens of our clan search out these places and attune with them through the use of ritual and trance work.

Many witches still hold to the ancient belief of animism, the basic concept being that all things in the natural world have a spirit and a destiny to be played out by fate. It is the belief among the witches of our clan that the ancestors reside in the landscape around us; the trees, the rocks, even the soil itself. There is a part of the spirit that merges with the natural world upon death. This essence dwells in the natural places of the world lending to it the gifts of memory and presence or feeling of spirit. Those spirits residing at a Nemeton are often worshiped as *genii loci* (pl.) where the ancients built shrines, altars and sacred wells to both honor and appease them.

The *genius loci* is in reference to *the spirit of a place*, usually a guardian entity that resides in a specified location. The term *genii loci* in its plural form is used in recognition of multiple spirits that reside in the same natural landscape; such places include forest glades or sparkling pools of water that often become recognized as sacred. *Genii locorum* is used in reference to a single spirit that has a larger territory. This means that a particular spirit is said to watch over multiple places which are usually in close proximity to one another. Sometimes this landscape has such powerful characteristics of spirit that its distinctive atmosphere becomes regarded as a muse for artists and witches alike.

The spirits of these places can be territorial at times; this can be felt by sensitive individuals who may stumble upon on the spirits territory or those who desecrate the landscape's natural beauty. In western Rome, there have been many spirit shrines found dedicated to specific land spirits. Among the Celtic peoples, deities were often linked to a specific location. There are several sacred wells that were built and dedicated to the goddess Bridhe, who is also associated with the Brent River. The goddess Boann is associated with the Boyne River and Danu who has long been associated with the Danube River where her followers would make votive offerings to her in the water. These places where part of deity's consciousness resides are also Nemetons. To the ancients, this consciousness was considered to be the *genius loci* of the landscape.

Alexander Pope wrote the following in regards to working with the *genius loci* in matters concerning gardening and landscaping;

> "Consult the Genius in the place of all;
> That tells the waters to rise and fall;
> Or helps th' ambitious hill the heav'ns to scale;
> Or scoops in circling theaters the vale;
> Calls in the country, catches opening glades,
> Joins willing woods, and varies shades to shades,
> Now breaks, or now directs, th' intending lines;
> Paints as you plant , and, as you work, designs."

6

Entranced in Manteia

I believe that witches should learn their craft and learn it well. To be a witch, one must experience witchcraft from all its many angles. One side of the craft that many witches today seem to ignore is the art of shadow crafting. The teachings of necromancy are often looked down upon because many witches today are misinformed about what necromancy really is. Many witches are also confused about the rites of the necromancer thinking that they must learn the arts of evocation to properly work with spirits. Yet there are others who have fallen prey to the propaganda that is produced by media, Hollywood, religious organizations and modern day Wicca. There is a real fear among today's witches concerning the use of spirits in magick; many are afraid of consequences that are more often than not based on superstitions spread by non-witches. This has caused the shadow craft to diminish. Many of its secrets have been lost to time and neglect by today's practitioners.

While teaching a class in Tampa a few years ago, I asked my group; "Does anyone know what necromancy is?" A young man spoke up and said; "Yes, it's something that no one should ever do!" It seems that like most people, the word necromancy instantly conjured an image of some dark magician summoning demons in this man's mind. I think he was quite surprised when he learned that the word necromancy refers to a form of divination and is not about controlling spirits, but rather divining the future or the past with the aid of the spirit realm. I must admit that shadow crafting is often used for other magicks involving the dead; however, this does not imply that these arts are harmful to the practitioner. All forms of magick have the potential to be dangerous. Those reading these pages should be advised that witchcraft is not for the faint of heart.

Some witches today, as well as those in our clan, are taught ways to work with spirits beyond communication. The witch necromancer has the ability to summon spirits of various types and work with them to attain certain goals. Some witches do seek control over spirits to carry out their bidding. When a witch performs such magicks, they are usually using a spirit as a fetch.

While magicians and sorcerers perform rituals of evocation, forcing a spirit to physically appear before them and then coercing it or threatening it to do their bidding, witches don't normally practice this type of ritual. A witch has a different philosophy concerning spirits, ancestors and their use in magick. A witch does not need a spirit to manifest in the material world. Witches are trained in the psychic arts, as well as various forms of divination. As such, working with spirits is often more mental than "magickal."

Most witches do not usually threaten a spirit unless forced to do so. Many are working with familiar spirits, elementals, and ancestors. Witches working with angels or daemons are often using the rites of evocation which are different than the rites of the necromancer. As such, the witch does not trap or restrain a spirit unless the goal is to imprison it in servitude (such as a fetch) or banish it by removing the spirit altogether. To truly understand the arts of shadow craft we must break its practices down and then look at it as a whole. We shall start with necromancy, trance work and communicating with spirits in this chapter. In the next few chapters, we will discuss how to work with spirits in ritual and discuss some of the inhabitants of the underworld.

The word necromancer has two derivations. The first is Greek, *nekromanteia*, meaning "one who uses corpses for divination." The latter, is Latin, *nigromantia*, meaning "black art". Because of the later, many people have come to associate the necromancer as one who controls spirits with black magick, or it is simply used by nonpractitioners to imply that all magick relies on such black arts.

The derivational suffix -*mancy* is often misused by many people including practitioners of the arts. In Middle English, it is *manci*, while in Latin it is *mantia* and in Greek, we find *manteia*, all of which mean divination. Words deriving from this suffix include- alomancy, cartomancy, geomancy, pyromancy, hydromancy and of course necromancy just to name a few. There are literally hundreds of types of divination that include the suffix -*mancy* in their names to specify a form of prophecy.

Originally, necromancy made use of human or animal body parts as a way to speak with the spirit realm and perform some divinations. Haruspicy, as used by the ancient Romans was a way of divining the future by reading the entrails of a sacrificial animal which included bulls, sheep, and poultry. Those trained in the arts were called haruspices, and would often read omens by examining the liver of a sheep. Today, the witch as necromancer may speak with the dead through the use of devices such as pendulums, dowsing rods, talking boards and automatic writing. Those in our clan are taught to use psychic ability, trance work and ritual to speak with the ancestors and other spirits.

Trance has always been used by witches to contact the gods, the ancestors and other spirits such as the *genii loci* of a specified area. Witches will use trance as a means of divination, channeling information from beyond the veil or to aspect divinity. Sometimes this includes the assumption of the god form. For those new to our clan, trance work is often met with some hesitation. Entering a trance may seem difficult the first time, but it is really a natural process that happens or begins to happen to us at nighttime as we slip further into the realm of dreaming.

In some cultures, ecstatic dance is used to enter a trance or hypnotic state. This is common practice in voodoo as well as in some tribal cultures were the shaman performs a ritual dance to enter into a trance state. While in this trance, the shaman or voodoo priest is sometimes ridden or possessed by spirits to allow the dead to speak through them. The motion of the dance distracts the brain so your conscious mind can be set aside. These rituals are designed to allow a spirit or deity to enter into the priest's body which then fills the gap that has been created for a short period. As the priest moves, they find that noises such as chanting, singing, and drumming become distant. They have entered into a dream type world where one may feel lost and at home all at the same time.

To understand trance as our clan practices it, we must distinguish between states of consciousness. Just as the hermetic philosophy teaches that all things vibrate, we find through science that our brains pulse and vibrate. This pulse can be measured in cycles per second and categorized as beta, alpha, theta, and delta. The first of these categories, beta, is the dominant pattern that we experience during our everyday activities. This beta wave is connected to the conscious mind; our rational thoughts and patterns. The second category is alpha, the pattern which we experience when relaxing for long periods, day dreaming or performing light meditations. Alpha is the state that witches train in to discover their witcheries and latent psychic talents. Theta is associated with extrasensory perception and trance work. Here we find dreams and astral travel, channeling and sometimes mediumistic activity. Delta is the state in which we find deep sleep and possibly access to the superconscious.

There are several ways to enter a trance state. We have already mentioned the well-known dance techniques of exhibitory trance work. As witches, we rarely use this form of ritual to induce the altered state of trance work. We do make one exception however in using a minor ritual called *seething*. Seething is used here to mean repetitive motion to enter a minor trance. This may be achieved when working in a coven by circling a central point such as a bonfire, altar or stang. When the witch is working alone, he or she produces the effect of trance by seething with a loom, staring at the spinning wheel as he or she pedals the machine into constant motion. Modern witches perform seething by rocking back and forth at an even speed on their own or with a rocking chair. This is naturally relaxing to most people but can be made more so by dimming the lights and staring at a fixed point without breaking concentration. Seething will not usually produce the projection of the astral body, but it can allow the witch to obtain clairvoyant visions, channel information or simply delve into the deep areas of the mind. While seething is a form of exhibitory trance, it is much less stressful than the ecstatic dance used by others.

Perhaps the easiest way witches enter a trance is with the use of herbs. While witches and shamans both use herbs to induce the trance state, the biggest differences are the types of herbs used and the way they are administered. Shamans often use herbs that are singular such as eating peyote buttons which cause hallucination and make a controlled journey almost impossible. Witches usually do not take herbs orally unless they are being used for medicinal purposes. Witches are taught to use herbs for trance work in combination, making them into oils, ointment, and potions which are then rubbed into the skin of the forehead, thighs and sometimes under the arms.

Herbs used this way can open the psychic faculties of the mind. However, this is artificial in nature, and the witch should train first to enter the trance state before using any herbal aids. This way the witch develops the skill of entering a trance and does not become reliant on herbal or artificial elements to force a trance state. Most of the herbals used in these formulas are meant to cause relaxation or slight intoxication. Some formulas will also make use of herbal components that are symbolic as opposed to being used for their chemical reactions. Sometimes witches will add components of the animal variety to their ointments in small quantities. These usually include animals associated with the underworld such as ground up crow feathers, fur from a black cat, skin from a toad or fat from any animal that is connected to the lower realm of the ancestors.

Among the covens in our clan, it is required that all

members must be taught the process of trance work as performed by the clan oracles. The function and practices of the clan oracles will be discussed in detail in a later chapter "The Covenant." There are two basic types of trance; a light trance and a deep trance. In a light trance state, the coven member is in between the alpha and theta states. In this light trance state, the witch is aware of their surroundings to some degree. This usually happens when the individual does not fully "let themselves go." This is actually very common for most witches when they first learn this process. For many students, the technique of trance work is challenging, and they may never get over the fear of letting go enough to perform the oracle position properly.

The second type of trance, the deep trance state is when the witch enters into a theta pattern. In this deep trance, the witch becomes mostly unaware of their surroundings and loses most of the feeling in their body. This is the desired state for oracle readings when channeling information. The best oracles are those that can let themselves go enough to enter this state while verbally communicating messages to the coven. While in this state of mind two things may happen; the witch entranced may reach into their own subconscious and deliver pronouncements and prophecies that their group needs to hear. This is the most common form of trance work that beginner students perform. Alternately, the witch may become partially possessed by a carefully chosen spirit which then speaks through the witch, using his or her mouth as its channel to communicate with the coven. This is the work of initiated clan members who have become comfortable with the trance technique we use and begin to delve deeper into the mysteries of this work.

For some coven members who are new to this process, it can be both frightening and impressive when witnessing a witch who is possessed in-trance. It is not unheard of for those under the control of a spirit to wiggle around a little or sometimes a lot, to use strange movements or possibly contort their bodies to some small degree. Other times the witch in a trance may begin to make strange noises, moaning or growling, speaking in a different voice or having their eyes roll into the back of their head. While this may sound demonic to some or fantastical to those uninitiated, this type of activity is not necessarily proof that the person has been truly taken over by the chosen spirit. The real proof comes from the accuracy of the messages delivered. Unfortunately, most of what is said relates to future events (however, not always) and so waiting becomes part of the process.

It's difficult to describe exactly what it's like to be in a trance state. Unless you have been in one, the experience can sound alien to most. Being entranced is like being in a dream state. You will most likely feel distant, relaxed or intoxicated, and only slightly aware of what you say or do. You may feel as if your body is out of control or unimportant. You may, or may not get the sensation of being controlled by external forces (this is more common in the ecstatic types of trance). I myself have described the deep trance state to others as feeling far away. Like being at one end of a stadium and hearing the voices of my coven as if they were at the opposite end. I also get cold and feel physically week with my body going mostly limp. When returning from a deep trance, I often feel otherworldly for some time after. Others in the clan, myself included, had mentioned that when you first open your eyes after being entranced, the candles used in ritual often make the altar appear as a blazing bonfire when first looked at. This usually causes those "awakening" to squint in discomfort.

Personally, having performed the mentioned trance techniques, I have given accurate clairvoyant and clairaudient
advice to the coven months in advance concerning the
weather, the harvest, a forest fire, and the death of a clan
member's relative, the birth of three different children, a
marriage, illnesses and more. However, there have also been
times that those things I have seen or heard in-trance have
not come to fruition and there has been a hand full of times
that what I said in-trance was either inaccurate or inaudible.
Trancework, like any psychic or intuitive process, is not a
hundred percent accurate all the time.

While in a trance one year at Samhain, I channeled the Celtic god Cernunnos giving him access to speak through my
body. I was told later by those in attendance that I growled
slightly at certain intervals, and my voice changed becoming deeper and harder to understand. I have witnessed other
coven members myself do odd things while in-trance as
well.

One year during Lughnassadh, I watched as the coven oracle clenched her hands tightly as to make a claw type shape.
She spoke with frustration in her voice and prophesized the
departure of several clan members. She then went on to say
that there would be a baby born to one of the coven members soon. Since no one was pregnant at the time, we were
all more than a little confused. However, this did, in fact,
happen about two months later. Several clan members left
the coven unexpectedly, and we ended up with new members shortly after. One of these new members was pregnant
and gave birth a month later.

The witches in our clan become proficient with trance as a
form of necromancy in order to receive and deliver messages from the spirits. Many of us witches create spirit shrines

in our homes in honor of their personal ancestry, or they dedicate the shrine to the spirits of witchery, possibly the genii loci of their surrounding area. Spirit shrines usually include cerain items such as skulls, feedings bowls and candles.

Skulls are a necessity in our tradition when working with the dead. Of course, in the modern day, finding or even buying a human skull is hard and expensive. If you have one, that's great! If not, you can always buy a fake skull from the store around Halloween time. Ceramic skulls are usually available. Gemstone skulls are also available year-round from gemstone dealers. You can also make a skull from clay if you want. However, you wish to do it is up to you.

Animal skulls work perfectly for these rituals also as they carry with them the memory of death as well as the energy of the totem you are using. Shrines with animal skulls are often used to contact a specific deity or totem animal for divination. Another advantage is that real animal skulls are much easier to find. You will need to choose one skull to be the focal point of your shrine. This skull should be the primary one used from this point forth.

When choosing a skull for this type of shrine make sure that it is intact. For divination purposes, the skull used should have the bottom jaw attached. This ensures that the spirit will be able to communicate with you from beyond the veil. If you are able to hear the spirits and a name is revealed to you, you may wish to call the skull by that name or create a sigil of the name and paint it on the skull.

Feeding bowls are used indoors to collect your blood. There is usually one bowl per spirit shrine or necromantic altar. The witch uses these bowls to collect their offerings of bloodletting with the shelg, bone knife or medical lancet (unless the witch is offering the *Blood of the Red Rose or Red Dragon*). These offering bowls are placed upon the working space for three days and then released outside. The bowl should be cleaned and replaced on the altar or shrine.

White candles are used to communicate with the dead. If your shrine is dedicated to one spirit, in particular, you may decide to simply burn one white candle, or you may want to add extra energy by having several white candles lit. Your shrine might not be dedicated to a specific spirit. In that case, you will be penetrating the veil with your mind and listening to the voices from the beneath you in the underworld, of which there are many. This is sometimes referred to as *Vox Esset Umbrae,* the "*Voices from Shadow.*" In the shadowy realm of the underworld, we can hear the ancestors speak through us, their voices coming to life once more.

With the shrine candles lit and incense designed to call upon the ancestors burning upon a charcoal, the witch should now entrance themselves in manteia. Anointing the mind's eye with Green Fairy Oil (or another trance formula) and fumigating your person with mugwort herbs you should sit in front of your shrine comfortably with eyes closed and begin to focus on your breathing. Start with your basic relaxation method until your body is limp and your mind is relaxed. With this basic relaxation accomplished, you will now go deeper into the darkness of the mind where the portal to the underworld awaits. The following is a simple technique you may try to begin a basic trance:

Visualize yourself standing in a room. Before you, there is an archway leading into darkness. As you walk into the blackness, you see a ladder that leads down. You begin to climb down the ladder one rung at a time going farther and farther into the void. With each rung you climb down, it seems that the bottom gets farther away. You know that the only way to reach the bottom is to let go of the ladder. You loosen your grip and fall backward down into the darkness of the underworld.

At this point, you should be in the beginning stages of trance. From here you will receive messages by allowing the mind freedom from the tight grip of the conscious mind. Unless the goal is to allow a pre-chosen spirit to speak through you, the witch should allow any information residing in the deep recesses of the mind to come to the surface. The mind is capable of prophesy while entranced this way and information can be gathered concerning all manner of things. The witch should have no preconceived ideas however in regards to what may bubble to the surface.

If, however, the goal is to allow a spirit access to the mind and possibly the body, the witch needs to allow the entity to speak unrestricted. In my experience, I have never had an entity harm me in any way while using this technique. I have however had a few spirits that pushed my body to bend or move in ways that I normally would not do so.

 Of course, trance work is only one way to reach into the spirit world. As a witch, the use of a pendulum should be second nature to the practitioner of manteia. Following the same beginning steps, sitting before the altar or standing over it, the pendulum can be used to contact the ancestors or to allow a chosen god or goddess to be channeled.

7

At the Crossroads of Night

In the dark of night, the witch who stands at the crossroads of the worlds shall find the answers they seek and the power they need. Down this road and in this place the witch finds that they are alone and in between the worlds, they find themselves in a place that is not a place, and a time that is not a time. Standing at the crossroads, the witch gains perspective into the realm of night. At the center of the crossroads, we find choice, decision, and possibility. One must enter the path and walk the road to find their way. On this journey, one may find the denizens of the darkness, the rulers of the kingdom below whose presence can be great and yet can be confounding. These ancient ones speak words that may twist the mind and act out in ways that can seem frightening to those uninitiated in their ways. But with this said, there is often, but not always, a truth of sorts that spills forth from their crooked tongues.

At the crossroads, we come to an intersection of choice, like a highway we may traverse one place for another. It is here that we become challenged, confronted by our inner demons. This can lead to the discovery of magick and will reveal much about ourselves as we commune with the spirits of the nightshade realm, but also by ownership of the deep-rooted dragon that dwells in the hidden places of the mind. Standing in the center, we find the convergence of the powers like flooding rivers that rush towards us. It is the practitioner who must stand his ground and become one with these great forces as they merge and mingle together becoming transformed and made anew in the center of the crossroads.

In folk magick, the crossroads are used to represent liminality, a place where we may find ourselves between three or more realms. There are many names for the deities that dwell in and rule over the crossroads. In Vodou, we find Papa Legba and Kalfou. Other names used for the spirits of the crossroads are Esu, Ellegua, and Nbumba Nzila. When one wishes to meet with the loa at the crossroads, they often do so at midnight or sometimes during the rising of the sun. It is appropriate to leave offerings of respect and gratitude for these spirits when asking them for advice or when trying to make a bargain.

The crossroads seem to have an even older history of use in European lands were the people of Greece would place stone markers in the center of the intersection. At these forks in the road, the people would honor the god Hermes, who was a traveler and explorer in both the physical and otherworldly realms. The people of Greece would often placate Hermes who they would beseech during short distance travel asking for safe passage.

The Greeks also associated the goddess Hecate with crossroads that converged in a "Y" shape intersection. At times the people would erect poles here and leave the goddess offerings of food. This was often done with prayers asking Hecate for guidance when someone was about to make an important decision. These people put their trust in her knowing that she would help them in picking the right course to follow.

Hecate is often associated with the moon as well as cemeteries. This goddess is also associated with the torch, possibly seen as symbolically, or literally, leading newly deceased spirits to the entrance of the underworld. The torch in this sense would be a sort of guiding light for the spirits to follow through *Ad Terram Tenebrosum*. The torch-bearing goddess is also said to have three heads, granting her the ability to look down all three roads simultaneously. We can see from this that roads leading out of town, where two or more roads crossed each other became the Pagan and folkloric altars of old. As the villagers of old would do, so too does the modern witch make use of the crossroads in his or her sorcery. It is here that we may speak with the ancestors and cast spells by joining with the current of the lower realm. The center of the converging roads becomes our altar, the axis mundi of the worlds where we light our candle and throw the stones.

The stang and the staff that witches use today embody these same characteristics, containing within itself a form of crossroads energy. The stang (and staff) is a magical link to the *"tree of spirit"*, sometimes called the *World Tree* by some or the *Tree of Life* by others. The stang mimics Bile and Yggdrasil for us here in the micro cosmos. Both of these spirit trees act as a central point between the worlds where their many branches and roots stretch out like roads into and out of the various planes. The intersection at the crossroads is used by the witch and sorcerer as a portal to other dimensions, if one would call it that, much like the staff and the stang. The witch who carries the stang is taking with him the power of the crossroads.

Before we get into the rituals, let us talk about some of the tools and devices that the witch should acquire. Spirit lamps are often used by witches when working with the dead. Like the torch of Hecate, these lamps are usually black metal or copper with glass sides. They are used to hold a white ancestral candle or a corpse candle depending on the work to be done. The witch may simply use an unscented white candle anointed with red wine or ancestor oil. Spirit lamps that have a black candle in them are only used for cursing or controlling magick. Some witches use copper bowls filled with oil as their spirit lamp. If this is the case, then the bowl needs to be fixed with chains so that the lamp can be swung when needed (similar to a swinging censor).

All witches should learn the skill of making candles, if for no other reason than to make their own spell candles. One of these candles that the witch should make in order to perform the rites of the dead is what our clan calls corpse candles or ancestor candles. Corpse candles are (usually) pillar shaped candles that are colored white, gray or black, being colored appropriately as the witch's needs call for. As the wax is melting, the witch needs to add graveyard dirt, powdered mugwort (or rue) and myrrh essential oil if making a white or gray candle. The witch adds graveyard dirt, powdered wormwood, powdered coriander, shredded skin of a snake and myrrh essential oil when making a black corpse candle. Regardless of the color, when these candles are cooled and hardened the witch should rub a small amount of animal fat on the candles. Since you can't refrigerate these candles, you will need to use them soon or wait to add the fat just before you're going to use them.

Some witches make and use corpse candles from the stalks of the mullein plant, turning them into torch style lights. This is accomplished by cutting a white cloth into long strips and soaking them in oil. When they are done soaking, the strips are wrapped tightly around the Mullein stalk. The witch then adds animal fat around the cloth and covers it with wax. These torch style corpse candles are placed around the ring to burn during outdoor necromancy rituals.

The bone knife or *shelg* should always be present for these rites even if they are not used. It's their symbolic meaning and sacrificial energy that is important. I was taught to use a specially made wand for the rites of the dead. The necromancer wand, if you like to call it that, should be made from a carefully chosen wood that carries the death energy in its branches. You may also like to make a wand from animal bone to be used for these rites if you prefer. Some witches use a dagger that is black from the handle to the tip of the blade. Others who perform a more Greek or Roman style ritual may use a knife made from copper. Again, I was taught to use a wand, but I leave this up to the witch to decide.

A scrying device is suggested for rites of necromancy if you wish to speak with the dead without entering a trance state. If your coven is fortunate enough to have a medium among its ranks than the scrying device may not be needed for group work. Of course, we are not all mediums, so, a black mirror is suggested to have on hand. Some witches may wish to make use of hydromancy for the communication aspects of their necromancy rituals. This is usually done with the cauldron or a black bowl filled with water. There are many rituals of the dead that do not call for scrying at all. The witch may be performing a ritual in order to ask for the aid of the spirits in healing, protection or retribution.

Careful preparation of ancestral incense powder is a requirement. The incense should be carefully blended in a quiet environment. There are two ancestral recipes that need to be prepared. The first is used to arouse the spirits of the dead to come and take notice of your working and the second is used to release those spirits from your environment. These incense formulas should be blended in a darkened room lit only by a single candle. This incense is best prepared during the disseminating moon, and if the luminary is in a water sign, that is better yet. If the ritual carried out is for a specific deity than that incense would be added to a burning coal just before the invocations are to take place. It is always best to think of safety and make sure to have some banishing agents on hand.

Sage is a low powered banishing agent that can move some minor spirits away from your person temporarily and is always good to have on hand. The banishing incense given in the Clan Formulary (Chapter 14) is a stronger blend used for a multitude of spirits and should be kept on hand during the rites. As a last resort, asafetida powder, sometimes called devils dung and favored by magicians, is known for its strength in exorcism. The magus usually keeps this powder under the altar or, in a box upon the altar, just in case the spirit summoned gets unruly.

Sulfur, a pungent powdered component related to the fiery energies of Mars can be used as a banishing or as an invoking agent. Sulfur burns rather quickly and can produce a brilliant blue flame when burned in ritual. This component is most often used to banish spirits and for hex-breaking. However, sulfur is a powerful mineral and can also be used in summoning spells and invocations to contact powerful spirits. It should be used with caution.

One of the key components in ancestral magick is the offering. A special plate or bowl (or both) will be needed. The bowl is used to collect liquid offerings such as wine, milk, liquor and blood to empower the spirits summoned. The plate is used to offer the spirits food, gifts, and other treats. If done correctly, the spirits will feed upon the essence of these offerings and gain enough power to communicate or act out your desires for a short time. Communicating with the spirits over time will allow you to know what type of offering each spirit will desire and what offerings may offend specific spirits.

There are some people who say that the dark rites of the necromancer should be carried out in the cemetery. The graves that are housed in the cemetery act as a connection to the current of death and thus make contact with the spirit realm easier for the practitioner. This is the basic idea behind the *Nekromanteia* of the Greeks as well; having the corpse on hand during the divination makes the connection to the spirit realm stronger.

The graveyard itself is one large portal with many entrances and exits to the underworld. The problem with this is that many sources indicating that these rites should be carried out in the cemetery at midnight were written during a time period when those authors would be less likely to be arrested for entering a graveyard after dark. For this reason alone working necromancy in the graveyard is usually best avoided. Instead, the witch should find a dark secluded place in which to work their rituals. Using the same location for these rites is also recommended as a portal will be built up over time.

There are several types of crossroads that can be created by the witch if they do not have access to the traditional "roadway" style crossroads of the ancients. We find it is easiest to use large bags of flour poured into bowls and mixed with dried wormwood herb. Once this is done a crossroads can be created with three or four roads by pouring the mixture upon the ground with an intense concentration of purpose. The three-pathway or "Y" shaped crossroads may be that of a triskelion, a Celtic symbol of water and the realm of Tir Nan Og. The four-pathway crossroad is shaped like a Celtic cross (without the circle), a symbol of the elements and the four directions. Once created, you may use either of these crossroads for a simple meditation. Begin by lighting the spirit lamp and reciting a prayer to the dead. Now enter into the center of the crossroads, the nexus of convergence and begin your meditation. You may decide to perform simple divination here as well including runes, hydromancy or pendulum work.

A Spell to Receive a Vision

When the moon is full and bright overhead and in the 4th, 8th or 12th house, take your spirit lamp, a clean white taper candle, a bottle of Green Fairy oil, and an offering of honey to the entrance of your crossroads.
Standing before the entrance of the crossroads, light the spirit lamp while repeating:

> *Spirits of the ancestors, spirits of old,*
> *Guide my path down the devil's road.*

Make your way to the center of the crossroads and sit. Taking your white candle, begin to anoint it with green fairy oil from the bottom to the top. Now using the ground as a candle holder, work the candle into the soil and light it.

As the candle's flame begins to fill the crossroads, anoint
your forehead while saying:

Spirits of the roads and the fairy-race,
show me the way to the sacred hollow.
Teach me this place that is not a place,
for you shall lead, and I shall follow.

You should now enter into a trance state (described previously). While in your trance there needs to be light concentration concerning your desired questions. It cannot be said
how long this may take. It may be moments, or it may be
hours. You most likely will receive your answers and much
more if you are proficient with trance. Before leaving you
should give a gift of honey as an offering to the spirits of the
crossroads.

To Cross an Enemy

This spell is best performed during the Balsamic Moon or
the Dark of the Moon, and if it is aligned with the sign of
war or restriction, that is better still. For this spell, you will
create a four path crossroads made from flour mixed with
sulfur. You will also need a cup of red wine, a spirit lamp
with a black corpse candle, 1 black candle, 1 large iron nail
or railroad spike, a volt that belongs to your intended target
and a wand made from willow that has been sanctified
during the dark moon.

In the dark of the moonless night, the witch stands before
the entrance of the crossroads the witch lights the corpse
candle placed within the spirit lamp while repeating:

Spirits of the ancestors, spirits of old,

guide my path down the devil's road.

The Celtic cross, which is a miniature symbol of the cross-roads itself, is now traced in the air at the eight directions starting in the west. In the center of the circle, another equal arm cross is made using the sulfur and flour mixture.

The first line being drawn from west to east, followed by the second line being drawn from north to south. When this is done, the witch holds the volt to their forehead endowing it with concentration and vision. The concentration here should be that the volt and the person is one and the same, a smaller piece of the larger whole.

The volt is now placed in the center of the cross lying on the flour and sulfur mixture directly. The witch now lights the black candle placing it in back of the volt while saying:

> *I supplicate, invoke and call thee up my dark lord,*
> *ruler of the house of shadow, teacher of the art,*
> *you whom I share blood and spirit.*
> *Hear my words from deep within the hollow,*
> *I do curse and cross _____,*
> *for he/she has transgressed against _____.*

Lifting the cup of red wine, drink a good portion. With the left hand pour the remaining wine over the volt with the following words:

> *In the name of the Puck and the Bucca,*
> *my desires burn like the flame between your horns;*
> *my words echo from above to below*
> *in the realm of Elphame.*
> *Hear me, great ancestors of the black cauldron; I*

make this offering to you and those spirits that dwell in the land.

With burning desire and focused will, drive the railroad spike through the volt pinning it to the ground. Taking your spirit lamp in your left hand begin to circulate the spike and the volt moonwise about three inches or so above. As you swing your lantern speak:

Ego do tibi maledicam, superius et inferius.
Ab intra et ab extra.
Ab hac die usque ad ultimum. Erit
(I do curse thee, from above and from below.
From within and from without.
From this day until your last. It shall be.)

Leave all items in the crossroads and leave by a different road than you entered.

The Path of the Moon

As a coven, the rituals of the dead are performed in a similar manner to our other coven rituals. Unlike the spells given above, they are performed without the use of the crossroads. Instead, we work within the witches ring. The crossroads rites are intended for solitary work. The rites of necromancy call for the witch to walk the path of the moon while creating the ring. The path of the moon here refers to the widdershins or counterclockwise motion which when done correctly creates a spiraling motion downwards, thus opening the door to the underworld. Casting in this way makes the energies of the circle flow downward naturally so we can ride the astral waves into the underworld, or send things away from us to be grounded out in the lower realms.

The same can be said for rings cast in the opposite direction, sometimes called deosil or clockwise. This type of witch's circle can open the door to the upper world, the higher dimensions giving you access to different spirits and energies. Depending on the nature of the rite, we may cast the ring clockwise using its spiral to lead us up and out. When casting deosil, we are following the path of the sun and the sky. For rituals of the dead, we always follow the path of the moon, gaining access to the energies of the underworld.

The path of the moon allows us to work with those ancestral spirits of the earth, the moon, and the underworld. We may work with other spirits here as well such as totems, familiars and the fey creatures of the mound. Traveling the path of the moon also teaches us about the shadow self, the dark dragon of the mind that dwells in the shadows of the underworld. Just as we may channel energies or information from the upper world, we may do the same from the lower realm. It is here that we learn some of the lost arts of divination and necromancy, as well as the low magic of the baneful type, those such as- binding, banishing, cursing and more.

Aspects of the Rituals of the Dead

Here I will explain some aspects of our rituals of the dead in some detail. This will show how a group might work these dark rites together; these are intended as suggestions rather than dogmatic practice. These rites almost always take place outdoors during the Disseminating, Balsamic or Dark Moon phases.

The coven assembles and is led by the magistra who carries the spirit lamp to the working area. The coven signs the summoner's book one by one, and then enters the working area where the opening portions of the ritual are begun. The coven guardian anoints each coven member with an appropriate oil on the forehead and both wrists with the words:

> *May the ancestors under the mound protect you this night,*
> *May the spirits who dwell in the moon bless you,*
> *May the Horned Lord and the Dark Lady watch over you, their witch.*
> **Bendith Y Mamau**

The coven scion lights the ancestor candles or corpse candles on the altar saying something along the lines of:

> *Spirits of the Moon, Witches of the Land,*
> *I do bid you arise mighty ancestors, blood of our blood. Awaken now from the Black Cauldron of Souls,*
> *Come to us from beneath the hallowed hill,*
> *Join our covenant tonight as we walk beneath the Dark (Balsamic/Disseminating) Moon.*

As part of the opening rites of this ceremony, we take up the skull that rests between two lit candles and anoint its forehead with oil. The witch then speaks an invocation of

summoning and then breathes life into the skull from his/
her mouth into the mouth of the skull. The skull is then
returned to its place between the candles. The witch now
takes the shelg or medical lancet and offers the spirits blood
from one of the hands (determined by the coven ahead of
time) into an offering bowl that rests before the skull. As
the red offering is made, words similar to the following are
spoken

> *Spirit of our spirit...... return from the mound!*
> *Bone of our bones.........return from the ground!*
> *Blood of our blood...... burning with life!*
> *Flesh of our flesh......... cut from our knife.*
> *We offer the essence of the living to the spirits of Terra*
> *Umbrae, so that they may speak to us once more.*

If the rites being performed are designed to call upon a
specific spirit, then an appropriate link should be used as
part of the offering. For example, if the coven was working
with Old Hornie himself, the god of witchcraft, then a skull
appropriate for him would be used. For the Horned One, a
goat, bull, ram or stag skull would work best. Other offerings such as wine are then poured directly over the skull
instead of into the offering bowl. The wine should run off of
the skull, so it absorbs into the land itself. This is significant
because of the funerary rites used by our ancestors. When
the bodies of our kin are buried in the ground, a portion
of their spirit merges with the soil becoming part of the
earth itself. Thus we are making the offering to those ancestral spirits as well as to those denizens who reside in the
underworld.

At some point during the ritual the magister will move into
the center of the ring, with his staff held high he will invoke
the Horned Lord by speaking something such as this:

Betwixt, between, all things unseen,
we walk and dance, we chant and sing.
Around about, within, without,
for from within, is from without.
By bull and goat, by stag and ram,
I call upon the horned man.
God of Light with golden rays,
we witches call on sabbat days.

After the opening ritual is completed, the coven moves on to the nights working. This is either a form of manteia referring to divination or trance work or, it is spell work designed to call upon the spirit of an ancestor, a fey, a shade or possibly a totemic spirit.

One chant we have used in the past is called, "the Weaver's Chant." When the entire coven chants this, it creates a haunting harmony and is perfect for the rites of the dead. It is chanted as follows:

We are the flow, We are the ebb,
We are the weavers, We are the web.
We are the flow, We are the ebb,
We are the witches back from the dead!

∽

I will end this chapter with a chant that can be used while sweeping the ring for rituals of the dead. Usually, when we hold a coven ritual, the ring is swept by a few female members while others dance. The coven drummers will play in rhythm with those who are sweeping, and the coven guardian will fumigate the working space while chanting. When working those rituals previously mentioned, however, the tone is more subdued; we try to create a quiet atmosphere for trance work. In these rituals the circle is swept moon-wise by three coven members while the rest of the coven quietly chants together:

In this ring, we witches give,
we sing the song so you may live.
Around and round we walk the ground
and light the way, so it be found.
In the darkness of the night,
we call the spirits to our rite.
Around and round we walk the ground
and call you from the hollow mound.

8

Terra Umbrae

One problem we face in the modern day is that some witches and magicians perpetuate the idea that the gods are not real, that they are archetypes of the mind's creation. This has sparked many witches today to follow suit with this philosophy, and the debate is still being carried out; are the gods real or are they archetypes? Whenever I am asked this question by others, my response is, "Both"! Like many things, the truth is usually hidden someplace between. We teach the witches of our clan that the realm of Elphame is both real and that it exists in the mind as an archetype. Why must it be one or the other? One might travel by spirit through the door of the mind into this realm and encounter the Queen of Elphame. If our physical body is not present, does this mean that the journey is not real? If the queen herself does not materialize in our ring and make pronouncements when called upon, does that mean she is not present at our ceremony? For us the gods are real, but they also live in the depths of the mind where they teach us symbolic values.

The underworld and its inhabitants are known by many names and can be found throughout the world in the stories and writings of ancient Pagan cultures. The Irish Celts called the underworld *Tir Andromain*, which seems to be divided into four parts and is home to the Celtic gods and goddesses of the underworld as well as the ancestors. To the Celtic Welsh, the underworld was referred to as *Annwvyn* and has many similar characteristics to *Tir Andromain*. In Greek mythology, we find the underworld of Hades that housed the souls of the dead and was divided by 5 rivers. To the Norse, the underworld was named Helheim (or Hel). In all of these cultures, it is taught that the underworld is located beneath the earth in a dimension that resembles our own but also has many fantastical differences.

The underworld is also called, *Ad Terram Tenebrosum*, meaning the *"Land of Darkness"*, while the shadow veil that separates our world from that of the dead is named *Terra Umbrae*, or, the *"Land of Shadow"*. After our physical death, a part of our essence is transferred back into the natural landscape of this realm, while a part of our spirit is taken into the underworld. The part of our being that resides in the landscape lends to the belief of animism and is why some places seem to be alive with an eerie presence. When the spirit merges with that of the land, they often become guardians of a specific place, family or clan. These spirits of animism can be advisors for specific individuals who walk the fairy path of the witch.

The parts of our spirit that travel to the underworld are claimed by the black cauldron of souls where we are transformed and made anew. It is during this process that a part of the spirit may splinter and become what is called a shade. This shade is a mostly mindless shadow that roams the veil of *Terra Umbrae*, a dark memory of sorts that can be seen by witches and psychics at times and have been witnessed by cowans[5] when visiting haunted locations. In the shadowy land of *Terra Umbrae*, we also find the veiled goddess of witchcraft. She is the lady of shadow, half-light and half-dark, similar to the goddess Hela of the Teutonic tribes. The veiled goddess stands guard between the worlds of the living and the dead. It is she who lifts the veil at certain times in the betwixt places of the worlds.

The witch learns to work with the archetype of the Veiled Goddess in the same manner that the Wiccan learns to work with the triple goddess. The Triple Goddess as an archetype of divinity used by neopagans first wrote about in Robert Graves' book, *The White Goddess* originally published in 1948 by Creative Age Press. Since that time, the term triple goddess has come to take on a life of its own, as any true archetype does.

Here we will examine some aspects of divinity as they relate to the underworld. However, to the crafter, the gods are real, and although they do live in the mind, they also live in the body of the earth and the vast luminaries of the universe as well. The Veiled Goddess is alive in the realm of *Terra Umbrae*, just as the Dark Goddess is alive in the underworld and in the dark recesses of the soul.

The Dark Goddess is often called the Dark Mother, the Dark Queen or Black Anis among other names. It is this dark goddess that keeps the mysteries and wisdom hidden from those non-initiates and teaches only those who she deems ready to weave the arts of witchcraft. The Dark Goddess can be found in the black soil deep beneath our feet, yet she is also found among the vastness of space beyond the stars dwelling in the eternal night where she wears the stars like a crown upon her ebony head. The Dark Queen of night is

5   Cowan is an old term used to describe a non-magickal person

the essence that nightmares are made from; encroaching upon the fragility of the psyche she is the originator of fear, the hag that resides in the dark places of the mind. Still yet, the Dark Goddess is beautiful. She is transcendence and stillness, a paradox of the primordial universe.

Another archetype goddess of the underworld is the Blood Mother, sometimes called the Bloody Goddess. It is she who is the goddess of the blood oath at initiation, she who is the keeper of secrets and pacts within the clan and among witches who work their magicks in the secret places of the night. The Blood Mother is often envisioned holding a single red rose, dripping blood from its thorns, a symbolic image that links her to *Sub Rosa* and the witch's mark.

The archetype of the Horned God is as old as the hunter/gatherer of our ancestors, and yet it is still unfolding before our very eyes in this modern era as we are witness to the rebirth of witchcraft in societies across the globe. The Horned One in Celtic lands has been called Cernunnos by the Gaul's, Herne by the Brythons and Arrawn or Vindonos by the Welsh. In other parts of the world, the Horned Lord has been known as Janicot, Pan, Faunus, the Devil and Old Hornie. Many traditional crafters today call the Horned God Tubal Cain, Azazel, and Qayin.

As an archetype, the Horned God figure is a protector who bridges the worlds of the tamed and untamed, the modern man and the Pagan man of old. For non-witches, the archetype of the devil takes on a Christian form that can terrorize the heart and stunt one's spiritual growth. However, for witches the Horned God archetype is connected to sexual prowess and the masculine mysteries of the craft.

In the mythic cycle of the sabbat ritual, the Horned God is

ever present as well as ever changing. In his emanation as
an underworld god, the Horned One is Lord of the Dead,
the King of the Hollowed Hill who resides over the gate
of death and grants the soul entrance into the realm of *Tir
Andromain*.

It is during the beginning of the dark winter months that
the Horned Lord shall lead a host of fey in the Wild Hunt
flying across the sky as wraiths. Here we find the primal
totemic animals of the Horned Master out in droves among
the living, some in physical form and some as specters.

Most notably among these totems is the crow that watches
the living and communicates all that it sees to the host. The
stag that is sometimes referred to as a hart, is often hiding in
the forests awaiting the call of the master. The *Yell Hounds*,
white of fur and red of eye and ear, are spectral hounds
from the underworld realm that the Dark Lord has chosen
to lead the way by sniffing out the souls of those He has
come to collect.

The host lead by the Black God is that of the dark fey; elves
and dwarfs from the beneath the earth who are sometimes
named the *Svart Alfar* among the northern tribes. *Aes Sidhe*
(pronounced, Ays Shee) is the name given in Celtic legend
for a race of powerful beings with supernatural abilities.
In Ireland and Scotland, these creatures came to be called
fairies and sometimes elves. In the Book of Invasions,[6] we
find reference to these fey creatures as living in an unseen
or invisible world that runs parallel to the physical world
of man. In Irish, *Aos Si*[7] or, *"people of the mounds,"* were
believed by some to be ancestors, while others reference

---

6   The *Lebor Gabala Erenn*, The Book of Invasions as it is commonly
called today is a medieval Irish text that basically recounts the mythical "set-
tling" of Ireland.

7   Sidhe

them as spirits of nature and others yet seem to believe that the people of the mounds were gods and goddesses. Sidhe creatures are usually regarded as both beautiful and hideous by the Celtic people thus giving hints as to the disposition of these nature spirits.

The Sidhe were fierce guardians of their fairy mounds and other places that they dwelt in. The people of Ireland would often leave offerings to appease them and considered these places to be sacred; most of these places were off limits to the tribe's people. The mounds themselves are portals into and out of the underworld where the ancestors, and fey creatures could step between the worlds. Fairy mounds are sometimes referred to as "*hollow hills*" because it is believed that they are dome type structures, each one housing a specific clan of Sidhe. The fey creatures of the Sidhe are ghostly spirits that inhabit the mounds traversing between this realm and the underworld. However, they can take corporeal form at times causing chaos when roused or lending a helping hand when appeased.

In the subterranean depths of Elphame, we find Finvarra, sometimes known as Finn Bhrea or Fionnbharr; he is known as the *High King of the Sidhe*, and often regarded as the *Lord of the Dead*, the *King of War* and the *Enchanter of Mortal Women*. Finvarra can be a benevolent ruler as well, known to keep horses healthy and to ensure good crops for the people of the lands. Together with his wife Oonach (sometimes Una) as *Queen of Elphame*, they rule over the lands beneath the trees in great magical cities. Finvarra is known for playing beautiful and enchanting music in order to make mortals forget things such as the mortal world and the families they leave behind when trapped in Elphame for a time. He also teaches witches the arts of fairy divination.

Oonach is regarded as a beautiful and radiant queen with golden hair filled with sparkling stars. Oonach is especially gifted with glamour magick and teaches shape shifting and how to use your sexual energies to gain new lovers.

In Scottish and some Irish lands, the King and Queen of Elphame are known as Ossian and Neve. Ossian, which translates to "fawn," is the son of Finn Mac Cool and the deer fairy known as Saba (sometimes Sabd). Saba gave birth to Ossian while in the form of a deer, but the child emerged from her womb in the form of a human sidhe gifted with the bardic abilities of poetry. Ossian traveled to the lands of Tir Na'n Og where he married his queen Neve, also known as Niamh. Together these two sidhe creatures grant the gifts of fertility and safe travel to and from the underworld lands of the Sidhe.

While Saba was known to be a deer fairy who could take human form, another Irish fairy Flidais, was called the "*Mistress of Stags*". Flidais, sometimes named Fliadias, is the ruler of wild beasts and the herder of magical cattle in the underworld. Flidais is often transported in a chariot drawn by stags or cows.

Far Darrig or Fear Dearg is often a solitary fey creature that enjoys practical jokes as well taking human babies into the underworld and then replacing them in the mortal world with fairy babies or changelings. Far Darrig is sometimes translated as "red cloak, red coat or red cap" which it always wears. Far Darrigs can help you to escape from danger, or they may place you in danger when they are displeased.

In Celtic myth the underworld is home to many totemic animals, fey creatures and goddesses such as the Welsh goddess, Cerridwen and the Irish goddess, the Morrighan.

Cerridwen is known to us as the goddess of the seed and the grain; she is the sower and reaper of the harvest, Lady of the Moon and bringer of the autumn rain. Cerridwen is an underworld goddess, a harvester of souls and nurturer of spirits. At one time pagans believed that the spirits of the dead rested in the moon gathering their strength so that they could be reborn upon the earth. Cerridwen as a goddess of the moon is dualistic in nature. She is Cerridwen the white lady, represented by the full moon as well as being Graidwen, the dark lady of war represented by the new moon cycle.

Among Cerridwen's totems, we find the owl, the sow, and the hare. Owls are often associated with death and the underworld. When you see an owl with one eye open and one eye closed it is a sign that the owl is keeping one eye in the world of man and the other eye on the underworld watching the happenings of its inhabitants. Just as owls can see in the dark world of night, they can see into the dark places of a person's soul. Owls are often signs of curses or the cursed. Like the beautiful and graceful sidhe creature Blodeuwedd who was cursed by the gods into the form of an owl after she tried to have her betrothed Lleu assassinated. The owl is a bird of wisdom, prophecy and the darkness of the underworld realm where it serves Cerridwen as a messenger and fierce protector.

The sow and the boar are prominent totems in Celtic lore found in brass carved statues throughout the European lands. Held in high regard, the sow/boar was admired for its fierce fighting, intellect and was known as an underworld totem. Sacred to Cerridwen who is sometimes called *"The Sow Who Eats Her Young,"* the sow/boar in the lower realms teaches us tenacity and how to use our skills to our advantage.

We find in Celtic fairytales and folklore many stories referring to crows and ravens. In *"Survival of Belief Amongst
Celts,"* by George Henderson written in 1911, we find a story
written about the *Witches of Mull* who can turn into crows
and take flight. In the same book, George also states that a
departing soul sometimes took on the form of a raven. In
"Fairy Legends of South Ireland" written by Thomas Croker
in 1825, he states that "If a raven is present when someone
dies, it was said to be the Devil retrieving his or her soul."
The Devil today is often confused with the Christian Satan
who in times past was not the biblical angel, but was rather
an emanation of the Horned Lord himself.

The word for crow or raven in Latin is *corvus*, an avian
belonging to the songbird family that is known for its vocal
cawing and intelligence with problem-solving. Crow and
raven myths are found all over the world as these birds are
highly adaptable carrion creatures that can hunt, scavenge
and feed on the dead. Crows and ravens are always associated with the underworld and are considered to be messen-
gers from the lower realm. In the past, crows were believed
to be omens of doom and or death, as well as being the
totemic bird of the Morrighan.

One aspect of the Morrighan, the goddess Babd, was known
as the crow of the underworld. Her witches in Ireland and
Scotland were said to change shape into that of crows in
order to fly to the witches Sabbat as well as taking flight
beneath the earth into the underworld.

Badb, whose name translates as "s*calding, boiling, furry or
crow,"* was sometimes known as Badb Catha, *"Battle Crow."*
Badb, known as Bodua by the Gaul's would sometimes
wail and cry throughout villages, leading to comparisons
with the Bean-Sidhe (banshee). Badb appears in the Togail

Bruidne Dá Derga as a harbinger of sorrowful death prophesying the fall of Conaire Mór. This led villagers to believe that her presence was a sign of impending doom. When Badb was spotted, war and death were soon to follow.

The piles of corpses left lying in the fields after a battle was often referred to as "the Garden of Badb." It was her sister aspect, Macha, who would then gather the heads of the fiercest warriors for her collection known as "the acorn crop of Macha."

In the underworld, the spirits that Badb gathers take the form of crows and ravens who constantly scream for her pleasure, just like the goddess herself who would take flight over battlefields screaming among the corpses. Badb's black cauldron of spirits is a portal into and out of the underworld where she stirs the souls who await rebirth. It is said that when Badb tips over the cauldron of souls in the underworld that great plagues and disease will take over the lands signifying the end of this cycle.

9

Familiar Spirits

Anyone who has had the fortune (or misfortune) of meeting my familiar Onyx, would tell you that our bond is remarkable. We found him outside behind a store during the heat of summer one year. When I picked him up he was so small he could fit in the palm of my hand, and his eyes were just opening. While Onyx was small, I made every effort to spend time with him, feed him and play with him. He learned early on that "I was his human." It was obvious from a young age that Onyx had a wild spirit, a trait that I noticed with my first familiar (also a cat) years ago as well.

To say that Onyx didn't like company would be an understatement and my coven mates, friends and family were no exceptions. After our bonding rituals had been completed, we grew ever closer. Onyx would often clean me like a cat, even on my face. He would also ride my shoulders, climb me like a tree and then lay down, head at one end and tail at the other draped across me like a scarf. Sometimes we would do magick or rituals in this way as he had a real talent for hanging on.

When I would open the doors to the temple to perform magic or work on a project, Onyx would get excited and run into the room ahead of me. A familiar's job is to help the witch perform magic, but also to keep the witch safe. This is a sacred bond between the witch and familiar; to protect one another from danger both physical and astral. I would often perform magick while Onyx would sit on my altar and watch me. Sometimes he would patrol the room as if he were policing the temple to keep me safe. Other times he would make loud cat noises as I performed invocations or chants. I always thought this was his way of joining in, adding his energy to my magic.

Once when I needed to perform a banishing spell, I decided to work on the astral plane first. I entered the temple with Onyx at foot and began the process. As I sat on the floor in front of my altar, Onyx came over and stood on my lap. He did not move the entire time, make any noise or other disturbances. He stood and watched as if he were guarding my body as I traversed the inner planes. When my journey was over, I returned to my body. Onyx must have instinctually known that I was coming back; he hopped off me and sat on the altar continuing to watch me.

Another time after moving into my new house, I was sound asleep in my new bedroom with my familiar lying next to me (he really didn't give me any choice in the matter, he insisted on sleeping next to me at all times). As I lay asleep, off and dreaming some random dream, I suddenly found myself standing in my bedroom. I looked down and saw my body still lying in bed.

Immediately, the bedroom door opened and what I can only describe as a creature of some kind slithered in. This being had the body of a short, plump snake with the face of a human or humanoid. I looked at the creature with shock, as it, in turn, looked surprised to see me as well.

The next thing I remember was being awakened by loud noises. I jumped from bed to see my familiar hissing towards the door. My bedroom lamp was laying on the floor, heart pounding out of my chest I got myself together and started to smudge my house. My familiar did his job; he was watching me sleep, protecting me from astral nasties and warning me by waking me up.

By the time that Onyx was three years old; he became very protective of the house. He thought he owned the house and we were actually his guests who he allowed to stay with him. One day while I was at work, my wife was at home waiting for a delivery of oil to be made. Finally, there came a knock at the door, and she went to greet the man. It seems that she needed to sign some paperwork and so she invited him in. The man walked in the door, and she began to fill out the required document. Less than a minute later Onyx came running around the corner and leaped onto the man's jacket. He clung to the oil man hissing and growling. My wife did the best she could to grab Onyx off him and eventually locked him in the sun room. By this time the man had retreated outside, and when my wife asked him back in, he refused rather impolitely.

When I got home, my wife told me the story of what had happened. It seemed rather out of character for Onyx to do such a thing; even though he was aggressive at times, he wouldn't normally go out of the way to attack people for no reason. It's possible that there was something wrong with this man. Perhaps Onyx sensed that he was dangerous or that he had a history of violence. I've learned over the years that when new people come into my home, I always look to see how my animals react to them. Animals, especially cats are very intuitive, and it is always best to pay attention to their lead.

There are only a few ways in which one would gain a familiar. The animal may be gifted to a witch by the offspring of another witch's familiar, or the witch would send out a call in the astral world, and the familiar then finds the witch in some way. In either case, this animal is not truly a familiar until the rituals of bonding are completed.

This, of course, is assuming that the familiar wants to bond with you! If it doesn't want to bond with you, it will become apparent quickly. You may also find that your animal doesn't have a penchant for magick. Some witches want to make an animal their familiar, but that doesn't mean the animal is going to comply with the witch. The animal may reject the bond; it may refuse the psychic intrusion upon its spirit, or it may simply deny any and all offerings you try to make towards your goal. If this happens, don't try to force a bond with your pet.

Some witches have a desire to call their pet a familiar for no other reason than the love they feel for their animal. Many people have a loving bond with their pets and treat them like family. Many witches are empathic and feel a special connection to their animals because of the emotional ties that empathy can produce. However, these things do not mean that your animal is meant to be a familiar. It must also choose you.

Choosing an animal to be your familiar is tough. Your "choosing" is only half of the equation. Your familiar must also choose you, and it must want to be your familiar, and be protective of you above all other things. The animal must be drawn towards magick. If it is scared of magick or simply shows no interest, why would you want to have that animal as a familiar? It would serve no function for you as a witch. Is your pet a loving, caring part of your family that you are bonded with? Yes, at least it should be. A magickal partner that guards you, your home and that is psychically connected to you? No. The animal you desire as a familiar must want to be your familiar and take on those responsibilities willingly!

To choose a familiar, make sure to take your time and watch the animal. It must be a baby or at the very least a young animal of its species. Watch the animal for as long as it takes, even if this is days or weeks. This part of the process is crucial. When you are ready, sit down close to the animal and see how it reacts to your energy. Does the animal approach you? Shy away from you? Ignore you?

You should focus on the ones that are interested, not too aggressive, but also not overly shy or weak in spirit. Try to choose a familiar that has some leadership qualities. When the bonding rituals are complete, your familiar will become more aggressive, some become a little feisty or even mean at times. This is truer with strangers and less true with the familiar's chosen witch. Assuming that the animal is walking, running and seems to be in good health, you would want to start the bonding rituals and psychic exercises as soon as possible. This should begin before the animal reaches 6 months of age, preferably around 4 months for most animals.

In the days of widespread persecution of witches, it was believed that every witch had a familiar spirit through which he or she would cast spells, spy on locals or cause havoc in villages and towns. Sometimes, regular house animals were considered proof that a person was practicing the arts of witchcraft. Most commonly, these animals were cats, dogs, hares and sometimes toads.

Many stories relate to the witch using their familiar as an instrument to deliver spells such as curses, love spells, enchantments and even to blight a growing crop. Some believed that a witch and her familiar were so connected that they could feel each other's pain. Familiars in this way were seen as supernatural creatures, not common animals. A witch's familiar was considered dangerous and was not to be approached alone or at night. Animal familiars were sent out by witches to spy on their neighbors and other town folk. They would watch those people that the witch would tell them to spy on, then report back to the witch's house in the wee hours before sunrise to tell the witch what they had seen. Perhaps it was believed that witches could speak with animals or at least with their familiar animal in some secret language unknown to other humans?

In the Year 1645, Mathew Hopkins the self-proclaimed witch hunter general claimed to find a simple way of identifying a witch. Hopkins would use the same measures as given by previous witch hunters to make a claim against them. If those accused possessed a domestic animal of some kind, Hopkins argued that this animal was a sure sign that the accused was a witch and that the animal was his/her familiar.

In records dating from the 15th -17th century there are witnesses who claimed that the witch would feed their familiar in some unwholesome way. Often, it was believed that every witch had received a "*Witches Mark*" someplace on their body. The witch's mark was a sign of their supernatural powers given to them by the devil. In the mid-1700s the witches mark was considered direct evidence that the accused was a witch. This mark was also believed to be the means by which to feed the familiar. Some accusers reported that the witch would feed their familiar through a birthmark, mole, scar or third nipple.

There were also accusations that some witches would feed their familiar on their own blood from a cut on their body. When the familiar had finished feeding it would produce a bruise or witch mark. Many records seem to indicate that the devil himself was responsible for giving the witch her familiar animal. Familiars during this period were considered to be just as dangerous as the witch they served.

Some stories from this period can be confusing. Some reports state that a witch would actually change her shape into that of an animal, while others stated that it was the witch's familiar who was doing the deeds they had witnessed. This seems to vary depending on the region that the accusations occurred in. In addition to animals, it was believed that the witch often had a humanoid creature as a familiar. These familiar spirits could look human at times and appear as misshapen or deformed at other times. In some accounts, these familiars were labeled as demons by the god-fearing folk. Later, they came to be called imps. Some claimed that these imps were able to fly around at night with large bat type wings and perform services that their witch masters commanded them to do.

The witches of our clan are taught to acquire a familiar spirit in four different ways depending upon the witch, his or her personality and their individual needs and desires. The four types of witch's familiars are as follows:

-*The Animal Familiar:* This familiar resides in a domestic

animal, but will usually be recognized as having a wild spirit and often has a foul temperament.

-*The Wraith Familiar:* This familiar resides on the astral, being seen by the witch and other intuitive people as a humanoid wraith form.

-*The Witch Stone Familiar:* This is often a semi-precious stone in which a familiar spirit has taken residence.

-*The Grand Familiar:* This is a large natural rock that houses a familiar spirit, similar to the *genii loci* discussed in a previous chapter.

In regards to the animal familiar, what most people fail to realize is that the witch's familiar is not purely an animal. First and foremost, a witch's familiar is a spirit. A familiar is not an ordinary household or domesticated beast, but rather a spirit akin to the witch that is dwelling within the animal. These spirits have their own names, agendas, and motives; at times acting independent of the witch, yet bound by the soul by means of magick. The most common animals for witches to use as familiar spirits are cats, hounds, hares, toads and frogs, ferrets, mice, snakes, lizards and a variety of small birds.

In 1556, we find a document from the Chelmsford witch trials stating that a cat familiar by the name of "Sathan" was responsible for teaching witchcraft to four women who were accused of practicing the black arts. In 1656 during the Fairfax witch trial of one Jennet Dibble, it was believed that she was in possession of a large yellow bird that she called "Tewhitt" and acted as her familiar spirit. During the same trial, other witnesses claimed that they had seen Jennet change shape into a large black cat at will.

The most common of all witch's familiars is perhaps the cat or *Grimalkin* as named of old. Pyewackett is the most common name for a cat familiar by witches in England. Cats have been revered as sacred animals since the times of the Egyptians who worshiped the cat in the cult of the goddess Bastet. The cat was known as the Mau to the Egyptians and seemed to play a large role in its society. The Mau can be found in both paintings and statues and was often mummified. The temple of Bastet was found in Bubastis of Lower Egypt which now lies in ruins. When Bubastis was the capital of Egypt, many Pharaohs had included the cat goddess in their throne names.

When a witch works with an animal familiar in our clan, that familiar is referred to as a *magistrix*, meaning 'Little Master'. The magistrix and the witch bond with each other during a series of special rituals that takes thirteen moons to complete. These rituals must be carried out while the animal is young and the rituals must be performed consecutively if they are to work. As part of the ritual, the witch feeds the familiar small amounts of his or her blood. The magistrix is then given a secret name that only the witch shall know.

Witches and their familiars have an ability to see through one another's third eye. To accomplish this, the witch needs to be proficient in the arts of clairvoyance or at the very least naturally talented in this area. Many witches are naturally empathic, they have an ability to feel from people, places, animals and even plants at times, but this should not be confused with psychic vision. During the bonding period, the witch gains the ability to see through the eyes of their familiar, he or she should be able to see what their familiar sees. Some witches may be able to communicate with their familiars mentally as well. However, this is rare.

Some witch hunters, historians and modern day Wiccans alike try to claim that witches will sometimes have exotic

animals such as owls, wolves or other wild creatures as
familiars. While these wild beasts have been used as totems
by many cultures and pagan religions, they could not be
made into a witch's familiar for practical reasons alone. It is
most likely that these wild animals may be a type of wraith
familiar.

Witches who work with such wraith type familiars must
have psychic vision in order to see their spectral helper.
Often witches will become aware of this familiar by having a
series of dreams involving the wraith. Many times, the witch
will not understand this experience and may try to reject
the familiar spirit. If this happens, the wraith will leave for a
time and then come back to see if the witch has progressed
to the point of understanding. Only then will the witch and
familiar bond.

Looking at the records of the famous witch trials of Essex
County in 1582, we find that thirteen women were accused
of witchcraft as well as having sixteen (or more) familiar
spirits who were believed to have taught these witches
sorcery and the making of magickal charms. These familiars were ghostly apparitions each with its own name and
appearance as documented. In Lancashire 1616, we find
records of a witch trial involving a familiar spirit who could
appear and disappear at will. It was said that this spirit
would give the witches advice on creating magickal devices.

When a witch's familiar appears, the individual as well as
witnesses may think that the spirit is that of a human or
ancestor, but one needs to be careful not to fool one's self.
The familiar spirit which is sometimes called an imp or
puckerel is not, nor has it ever been a human. Even if it
appears to be humanoid in shape, this type of familiar is
a being of the underworld realm sent by the Horned Lord

and the Dark Lady to assist you in your sorcery. Don't be surprised if this familiar spirit appears after a ritual or after having visions of the Horned God. This is somewhat common for witches who have gained the attention of the Horned One or Black Anis. The underworld has taken notice of you and is now trying to send you aid in the form of a familiar spirit that will assist and teach you the ways of the craft.

This wraith type of familiar is bonded with during special rituals, much like a magistrix is. These rituals are usually best carried out during the dark of the moon or when the moon is aspected with the signs of Taurus or Capricorn. These rituals work best when the witch prepares a special receptacle for their familiar. This receptacle should have a lid of some type that the witch can remove in order to make a small blood offering to their familiar. Offerings done in this way, make the familiar stronger for short periods of time giving it the ability to become somewhat more tangible and gains access to the physical realm.

This type of familiar will often reveal its name to you after you make your first blood offering to it. A wraith familiar can take many forms. Don't be surprised if your familiar appears to you as a humanoid with wings, or long fingers. It may have yellow or red eyes; it might be quite short or extremely tall. The familiar spirit may take on the form of an exotic looking animal as well, but know that this is probably not the familiar's true form.

Your familiar will not harm you; it's there to assist you and work with you in your magickal operations. This doesn't mean that it won't act independently at times. Your familiar doesn't just sit around at your house all day while you're off at work. You may send messages to your familiar by writing its name down on parchment and burning it in your cauldron while speaking aloud what you wish it to hear. Your familiar may appear to you that night in a dream or in the smoke of incense. It may make itself known as a shadow on the floor or the wall.

Among the different types of familiars witches employ the stone familiar, or witch stone is a type of magickal helper. Similar to an animal familiar, witch stones are made from a specific form of mineral that the witch feels most drawn too. Each witch must make this decision and will then bond with that specific type of stone or crystal. The choice of witch stone usually reveals much about the witch and their forms of witchery (natural abilities).

Each witch stone you are in possession of should be anointed with your witch's blood. It should be realized by the witch that it is the spirit within the stone that you must bond with and communicate with in order to use it as a familiar for magical purposes. Witch stones are often worn as jewelry such as rings or amulets and are used to aid the witch in spell work by adding power to the witch's sorcery.

Unlike the animal familiar; the witch may have as many witch stones/gemstone familiars as he or she likes. Each one should have its own name, and you need to learn its personality in order to work with it and draw power from it. The gemstone familiar should be worked with on a psychic level first, only then should the witch anoint the stone with blood and give it a familiar's name.

The following is a list of common stones for the male and female practitioner in our clan. Of course, the list is not one hundred percent complete (they are simply the more common choices for the sexes).

Male witches often work with the following witch stones: amber, amazonite, bloodstone, carnelian, cats eye, diamond, emerald, jasper, malachite, onyx, ruby, citrine, serpentine, sun stone and tigers eye.

Female witches often work with the following witch stones: opal, pearl, selenite moonstone, sodalite, jasper, jet, onyx, amethyst, lapis, rose quartz, topaz, fluorite, appatite and falcons eye.

The *Grand Familiar* is similar to a witch stone but is a natural unpolished stone found on the witch's property or close to the witch's home. The grand familiar is often very large and is not meant to be worn or carried around. This familiar spirit links the witch to the *genii loci* of their surrounding area. It is a familiar of the witch's land that is brought inside. The witch names the grand familiar, creates a sigil and then carves or paints the sigil on the stone. It is then anointed with witch blood and kept in a special place in the home. Some witches make use of the dolmen[8] in a similar manor and don't use the grand familiar at all. Some witches have used extra-large crystals that they bury on their property for 13 moons. They dig it up and then bring it inside, and after completing their ceremony, they use this crystal as there grand familiar. This is not the preferred method, but it will suffice enough if the witch has no other options.

Whatever type or types of familiars the witch possesses, they are meant to be personal to the witch. Your familiar has no connection to your coven except through you and you alone. Working with familiars has become a dying art. Many witches today no longer know the rituals of making a familiar, others don't even know that they need to do such things to gain a familiar; instead, they acquire an animal and simply call it a familiar. Similar to the old stereotypes

8   Dolmen is another name for the altar or hearth stone.

that all witches have a black cat, many of today's witches believe it to be as simple as that.

10

Covenant of the Witch

It is believed that the word "*covenant*" did not appear in the witch trials until sometime in the year 1662 at the trial of the Scottish witch, Isobel Gowdie. At least it seems as though that's when the word first appeared in documentation. The word *coven* was used here to indicate that the witches of Scotland had made a pact to keep their practices secret, sharing their magickal information only within their group or coven. It was also used as propaganda by witch hunters of the time to denote that witches signed a pact with the Christian Satan to gain their powers.

The word *covenant* can be found in old French as *covenir*. In old English, we find *covene,* which eventually became *covenant.* If we look at Latin, we find the word *covenire.* All these words roughly translate to mean *agree, agreement* or *come together.* In the modern era, the term covenant has been reduced to the more convenient "coven." Not all witches work within a coven, and in the modern witch movement, there are more and more witches who practice without a coven, or without any training for that matter.

The word covenant is used as a pact between two or more people or two or more tribes. One may also look at it as a pact between a man and spiritual force. The word covenant is also found in the Bible. When witnessing a transaction, Jehovah was called upon, and the agreement was called "Covenant of the Lord" (Genesis 31; 50) (Samuel 20; 8).

In a witch's coven, the members are trained to perform ritual in various forms to strengthen their bond with each other, with nature and with the ancestors. Members are also trained in spell crafting to produce the manifestation of their desires. Witches in a coven are usually taught the mystical arts as well. These include psychic powers, astral travel, fascination, trance work and more. When witches gather in a coven, their power is magnified many times over! A solitary witch can only harness so much energy, but when two witches gather their energy is multiplied. While many would assume this energy would be doubled, it is in actuality quadrupled.

As covens go, there is usually a series of meetings that take place, some of which are for the purpose of ritual, while others are for spell casting, divination or for more practical reasons such as scheduling and decision making. Most witches practice Sabbat rituals as part of their gatherings.

⌇

Our clan is made up of a number of different covens all which operate independently yet are bound together as a family. It is the responsibility of each coven's leaders to maintain communication with the clan elders. Solitary clan members are responsible for maintaining their own communication with the clan elders. In either case, those members that break communication are no longer considered clan members until they make contact again. Every clan member must fulfill his or her blood oath to be an active member of the clan as a whole.

At some point during the progression of each individual, they attain mastery of the craft and are permitted to start a coven in the clan, if they wish. Doing so means that they and their coven (coven meaning "agreement") must obey the clan rules. Any time that a new coven is created within the clan it must meet the basic requirements of the clan laws as written. It must then be approved by the clan elders who have the final say concerning the coven name, deity, totem and so on.

To begin, the coven must decide upon a matron or patron (coven deity), who will then watch over the coven, guiding its members and setting the tone and feel for the group as a whole. This choice is vital and will affect those members that are drawn to your coven. It is often the coven's matron or patron who chooses the group's participants by testing the coven's potential members. The coven deity will also challenge the group at times; this may make some members flee while others stay accepting the challenge that they were given in whatever form it takes. This sort of weeding out process is not uncommon depending upon the deity the coven has dedicated itself too.

Our covens work with the Celtic pantheon when choosing a matron or patron; we feel that this gives us an overall sense of cohesion among the covens. My first coven in the clan aligned with a goddess that is known for her healing attributes, good disposition, and is considered to be charitable to those in need. Our first several members that joined the coven all worked in health care. We had a nurse, a doctor, a technician, a therapist and a nursing student among our ranks. This trend continued for a few years pulling in people who worked in health care or who were going to school for a career in medicine. I remember one year we held a ritual during the Summer Solstice and invited several members of various covens. All of those who attended the ritual worked in health care in some manner. Those witches who were unable to attend did not work in the health industry. The message of our matron was loud and clear.

At some point, a few years later this changed dramatically. Instead of pulling in new students who worked in the health industry, we started to attract those that needed healing. Most of the time this was emotional or mental, but occasionally it was also physical. We began to draw unbalanced people who were instinctually attracted to us. Our totem taught us the arts of healing in many forms and then wanted us to put it to use by healing some of our coven members. Over time this proved to be exhausting, and several members either left or were kicked out. Those who remained were our strongest coven members, and together we healed as a group, rebuilt our coven and continued on our path.

The second coven in our clan that I ran used a patron deity who had harsher qualities than the previous. This coven attracted members who were tough mentally and physically. We worked our rituals to near perfection and drew to us those who could do the same. When someone couldn't meet our patron's standards, they often left the coven for one reason or another. Those that stayed became initiates and eventually took over the coven. My time to leave was at hand, and I moved out of state forming yet another coven within the clan.

We believe that the oldest of covens use totemic animals to guide their group and its members in the practice of witchcraft. The totem that your coven aligns with says a lot about your group and their practices. The totem that is chosen must make sense for your group and should inspire your members to greatness. The best covens in our clan are those that make use of their totems strengths by practicing totemic magick on a regular basis.

Totem animals are used for meditation purposes as well as path working. This leads to the discovery of the coven finding its identity among the clan. However, on a personal level, it also leads the individual witch to discover much about the self. Through the use of totem magick, the witch learns how to connect with the totem to materialize those attributes that their totem exemplifies in the physical and spiritual world. From here the witch will move on to explore other totem animals and their many magickal attributes.

The totem spirit of any coven within the clan must match as a totemic animal of that covens matron or patron. Animal totems are often used to traverse the great tree known as *Bile*, delivering messages to the upper and lower world entities that reside there. Witches and their covens are taught to use their totem in this way. The totem can also be used to aid the witch in hedge-crossing and traversing the hidden pathways to the underworld realm.

Many traditional crafters wear black robes. Our clan members follow this tradition and wear black robes that are usually simple in design and must have a hood attached. Each coven in the clan must decide upon a secondary color when their group is first formed. This second color is worn on the robes by all coven members to designate which coven they belong too. This color also shows unity among the coven and should correspond to the coven's matron or patron. Most often this color is sewn onto the sleeves, hood, hem or all of those mentioned.

Covens may have as many initiates as they like. However, each coven must have at least one magister or magistra in order to be recognized as a coven in the clan. As a rule, if an initiate stays in their coven, they must take on students to teach, and they must assist in the training of all students within their coven. They may also be asked to help train students from another coven if help is required and the distance isn't too far.

The magister, or male witch priest, is a living representation of god energy. It is the magister who channels the god and becomes his voice on earth. In days past the magister was known to wear a horned mask upon his head. Sometimes the magister becomes the man in black for ritual. For us, this happens at Beltane and Samhain as well as at initiations. Any magister who runs one of our covens is called a *clan father*. He may take on students of either sex and train them in the ways of the clan. The magistra, or female witch priest-ess, is a living representation of goddess energy. Like the magister is to God, so the magistra is to Goddess. It is she who channels the Goddess becoming her voice on earth. In days past the magistra would paint her face appropriately for the season, or she might wear a mask or a veil during ritual depending on the occasion. The magistra in the coven is called a *clan mother* and may take on students of either sex just as the magister.

The coven has four major stations and a series of minor stations or positions of responsibility. Once a coven member agrees to fill a major station they are bound to that obligation for a year and a day. The council shall ask if anyone in the coven would like to try a station. Those who are already filling one of the stations are usually asked if they would like to continue for another year and a day. The council takes this into consideration and makes its decision upon their next meeting. The four major stations are as follows: the summoner, the scion, the oracle and the guardian.

The summoner should be at least a first-degree initiated member of their coven. The summoner may be a male or female but should be naturally gifted with organization skills. The summoner is the keeper of the *summoner's book* within the coven. This book is a written record of rituals, prophecies, initiations and other observances that the coven goes through. The summoner's primary job is that of a scribe. The summoner is the keeper of records, files, and rules within the coven and clan.

The coven scion should be a dedicated member of their coven. The scion may be a male or female, but they tend to be mostly female witches. The scion should be a naturally positive individual who brings energy and happiness to the coven gatherings. The scion is the bringer of light. It's their job to set the astral bubble of the temple; setting lights and creating a positive atmosphere for the coven to gather in. The scion usually recites prayers or charms while lighting the temple candles. She also leads the coven when the sweeping is performed. Also, the scion leads in spells for healing, success, love and other positive acts of magick such as blessings.

In regards to the oracle; it is preferred that the coven oracles be at least first-degree initiated members of their coven. The oracle may be a male or female but should be naturally gifted with psychic ability and intuition. The oracle's primary job is to keep one eye in the spirit world during rituals, making sure that the local and non-local spirits are appeased and not hostile towards the coven and its activities. It's recommended that each coven has at least one oracle, but it is possible to have multiple oracles in one coven if there are multiple individuals who have an aptitude for trance work or psychic ability.

The coven guardian should be at least a first-degree initiated member of their coven. The guardian may be a male or female but should be someone who is a natural protector or who has warrior type qualities. If the coven is large, they may decide to have more than one guardian. The main job of the temple guardian is to keep all members safe both physically and psychically. The guardian shall smudge the working space with sage or fumigate it with a stronger herbal blend during the opening ceremony. The guardian usually has a special bag tied to their initiation cords which is filled with banishing agents and protective charms. Most guardians have a number of banishing or protecting chants memorized.

The four minor stations in the coven are filled by multiple group members and tend to change as each Sabbat is performed. The four minor stations are; the coven healers, the coven drummers, the coven maidens and the coven burners.

The coven healers are any coven members who have a natural or trained skill in the healing arts. These individuals usually make use of simple candle magick, herb lore, folk remedies, and energy healing as needed. The coven healers will often lead in spells of healing. If there are no such healers in the coven this responsibility falls to the scion.

The coven maidens are uninitiated females of any age who

perform simple tasks during the ritual such as setting up the altar, dumping libations and other simple chores. The maidens perform the sweeping of the ring following the direction of the scion. Not all covens have maidens. If there are no maidens, these tasks usually fall on the coven summoner.

The coven drummers are simply those members who perform music during the ritual, especially during the opening ceremony. The coven drummers add needed energy to the gatherings. If there is no drummer, this station usually falls on the guardian.

Most covens have burners. However, it is not a must have station. The coven burners are responsible for acts of retribution that fall upon the coven or its members. The burners then gather together forming a temporary coven known as a *burner coven*. If there is no burner in a coven, this becomes the guardian's responsibility.

~

To understand how the stations work I will give two examples of the stations fulfilling their duties in ritual. During the opening of a coven ritual, each member signs his or her witch name into the summoner's book and then steps into the area where the working will take place. The coven members are then anointed on the forehead and the wrists with a small invocation of blessing. The summoner now recites the purpose of the gathering for the ancestors and spirits of the land to hear. The scion or guardian pick up the horn, usually from a bull, and blow loudly signaling the drummers to begin (the drummers and scion should decide the tempo prior to this). The maidens now sweep the area, led by the scion; they should sweep away any sticks, twigs or rocks that may hinder the covens movement. As they go around the ring, they chant a charm for the working. As they do this, the guardian follows behind them fumigating the area with an incense blend burning on a red-hot charcoal. This opening ceremony can go on for some time, only ending when the scion feels the energy is built up to the proper level. When she experiences this feeling, she holds her broom up over her head, and the drummers change their rhythm. The working space is now prepared.

During some Sabbats and Dark Moon rites, the oracle will perform prophetic work while in a state of trance. This is begun by the oracle (or oracles) drinking a specially prepared tea. The oracle is then heavily fumigated with mugwort herbs. The guardian then blindfolds the oracle who is seated in the west while the rest of the coven sits on the ground. The guardian stands behind the oracle who begins to enter a trance state for prophecy. The coven's scion now asks the oracle questions that have been prepared ahead of time. These questions usually pertain to weather patterns, crop growth or harvesting and other natural occurrences over a three-month period. After these programmed questions are asked, the coven may receive personal messages from the oracle if they desire. As the scion asks these questions, it's the coven summoner who writes these prophecies down in the summoner's book for safe keeping. Personal readings are never written down of course.

Hopefully, these examples give somewhat of an idea of how the coven stations work together. When everyone knows their job, and performs them well, the ritual goes smooth, and the energy is built properly. There is a rhythm to any ceremony, and when the witch works within that rhythm, true magick is made. There will be occasions when certain aspects of a ritual can be miss-timed; this usually results in other aspects of the ritual being thrown off and the coven can be thrown into a rhythm of chaos. The rhythm of chaos can be fixed if it is recognized in time but calls for experienced witches to bring the ritual back into balance and order.

11

Implements Of the Art

Before we go any further, we will need to discuss the tools
of witchcraft. We will discuss the implements that our
clan puts to use, as well as the basics of how we use them.
I will try not to repeat too much information here as there
are already several good books on the market that discuss
the tools of the witch and those of traditional witchcraft.
For additional information on the implements of the art
that we witches use I have included a full bibliography in
the back of this book. The tools of witchcraft do bare some
resemblance to those used in Wicca. However, some are
completely different, while others are similar but called by
different names or have a slightly different appearance.

The tools of witchcraft do vary from clan to clan. However,
there are several implements that seem to be used by most.
Among these more common tools, we find the broom, the
black knife, the cord, the cup and the wand. First, we will
look at the witch's broom.

The broom for us is often a simple wooden shaft that is fairly straight, yet has character. The shaft section is often made from a masculine wood to represent the Horned God. A traditional broom is shaped by the witch's own hand so that one end has a slight phallic shape to represent the God. It is a tradition among many covens that the phallic end of the broom is inserted into a female coven member to sanctify it in the name of the Horned God. The god symbol is then covered with bristles of plant material in a "V" or cone type shape to represent the Goddess.

The broom in modern Wicca, called a besom, is created by the initiate for the purpose of cleaning away negative psychic energy. The broom's purpose in our clan is both practical and magical. In Wicca, the besom never actually touches the ground as where our brooms are used to sweep away debris, sticks, twigs and other pesky intruders that may find their way into our working space. In a British Traditional Wiccan coven, the maiden will clean the circle in a sweeping motion while chanting "The Besom Song," she will then spin her way out of the circle. Again, the covens in our clan perform a different type of ritual. We have multiple coven members sweeping the circle and chanting a banishing charm as they follow the path of the sun or the path of the moon; depending on that night's working. As they do this, other coven members are drumming, and the coven guardian is fumigating the working area with a specially prepared banishing agent.

Among our covens, we teach our students to use their brooms (as well as their stangs) for astral travel. This does not imply that these two tools are required for the witch to astral travel. The broom or stang can, however, help the witch in their journeys if used correctly. I liken this to a car; you don't need a car to go to the store, you could simply walk. However, the car/broom makes the journey faster and sometimes safer.

The broom is also used in magick. The broom is often used for spells of cleansing and blessing as well as house blessings and the rite of Imbolc. The broom is also used for weather magick if rain or water is involved. An old witchcraft spell for calling rain is performed by gathering at a stream or river and beating the top of the water while chanting. If the coven is present, there shall be drumming as well. Chanting is obviously focused on invoking water and the spirits of the upper realm to produce rain for crop growth and in times of drought.

The broom is also used to drive rain, thunderstorms and high winds away from the witch's property in times of need. This is done by tracing specific sigils on the dolmen and burning an incense of banishment, then taking the broom in hand and sweeping the weather away from you and yours. Again, chanting is required, but this time focusing on sending the weather away.

A practice in our clan that we try to adhere to as best as possible is the keeping of the broom after a clan member has passed away. We try to collect the brooms of those who cross beyond the veil and keep them in their coven's temple against the northern wall. During our Samhain ceremony, we use the brooms of the dead to sweep the circle with, thus honoring their spirits in our ritual. This is the only time we use their brooms for magickal purposes unless we are performing the rites of necromancy to work with that specific ancestor.

The black knife is a personal tool of each witch, a receptacle of their personal power. The knife for us is a symbol of fire on the earthly plane; it is used to administer your willpower in sorcery and ritual. Our knives are always black. Black is used to draw and hold in energy that we then release consciously in an act of magick. Black represents the void of creation, the Horned God in his guise as Lord of Death and the Dark Goddess, she who stirs the souls of the dead.

Because the knife is forged in fire, we associate it with the blacksmith gods and the realm of Findias. It's a masculine tool used by all members of the clan. Like the other personal tools of the witch, the blade is also linked to you from your own blood taken from the finger of the sun.

The cord or cords in witchcraft seem to vary by clan, family or tradition. Often the cord is given at initiation into the craft and is used as a symbol of acceptance as well as an implement of sorcery. In witchcraft, there can be either one initiation or three initiations. Some witches belong to traditional covens that only have one initiation; if this is the case, that witch will only ever receive one cord as part of their elevation. If however, the coven does three initiations like we do, then there will be three cords made and given to the initiate; one for each degree.

In our clan, the initiate is given a white cord at the first degree. This cord represents the White Goddess of Fate found in the old craft, as well as the Horned God as a youthful springtime lord. Symbolically the white cord represents the maiden or son aspects of the human aging process as noted by Robert Graves, in his book *The White Goddess*. The white cord is also used symbolically to represent the *white thread* in hereditary witchcraft. This means that the individual has been adopted into the coven or clan and is treated like family.

At the second degree, the initiate is given the red cord. This cord represents the Horned God of witchcraft as a giver of life and fertility. This cord is also given for the Blood Mother, the keeper of craft secrets under the rose. Symbolically this cord represents the mother and father aspects of the human aging process as noted by Graves again. The red cord is also symbolic of the *red thread* of witchcraft, the bloodline or lineage of the ancestors.

At the third degree, the initiate is given a black cord. This cord represents Black Anis, Goddess of the Underworld and keeper of the Cauldron of Souls. The black cord also represents the Horned God as Master of Death and Lord of Resurrection. Symbolically this cord represents the crone and sage aspect of the human aging process as noted by Graves again. The black cord represents the final stage in the process, completion of training and the ability to teach others in the clan.

The cords of initiation can also be used in magick. The white cord is used for spells of healing, blessing, protection, and knowledge. The red cord is used for spells of passion, sex, fertility, growth, psychic magicks, ancestral workings, as well as reversal and protection sorceries. The black cord is used for protection, binding banishing, wisdom, ancestor work, divination and astral travel. The three cords are also representations of the three worlds; white for the upper world, red for the middle world and black representing the underworld.

The cord or *singulum,* as it is sometimes called in Wicca, is created and given to the new initiate as part of their elevation rituals. At the first degree, there are actually two cords made, one that is given to the student and one that is kept by the High Priest and High Priestess. This second cord that is made is given back to the student upon completion of their third degree. It is said that this cord would be used against the student in case he or she should betray the coven that initiated them. This singulum which is marked with the initiate's blood would be used as a volt to curse the individual, being thrown into a swamp or other place of decay to rot. The cords in traditional Wicca are also used to measure out the working circle.

The horn is often an underestimated tool in the craft. While some witches seem to make use of it, many others do not. For us, the horn is made from the horn of an animal, or from the bones of the dead, which may be either human or animal. When the horn is blown at the beginning of the ritual, it is done so to summon the spirits from the underworld and the fey from the hollow mounds.

The cup used in witchcraft is often made from clay. However, I have seen a few made from ceramic and stone. The cup is a plain looking drinking vessel used in ritual. It represents the ancestors, the underworld, fertility and the feminine. For libation magic, the chalice is filled to the brim with a liquid chosen for the working. This type of sorcery can be used to enter the nightshade realm. If done properly these rituals produce an altered state for trance working, divination and the oracular process. When performing libation magick, the cup is often surrounded by a triangle of fresh foliage that is chosen for its attributes of wisdom and divination.

I have seen many witches who follow the crooked path use a bullhorn as their cup. This brings a balance of masculine and feminine energy to the vessel. I must admit that I have a metal cup that I use for indoors rituals and a clay cup that is preferred for outdoors rituals. This is done, so I do not offend the fey creatures of nature when working outside. Most witches try to limit the amount of metal brought to a gathering in the forest.

When one meditates on the cup, you can see the obvious connection to the element of water and the hidden knowledge of the western gate, as well as the city of Murias. This is one clue as to the great power of the chalice. Another way to work with this vessels energy is by means of those feminine deities of love, intoxication, and transformation. It is best to sanctify one's cup on a Friday in the hours of Venus when the moon is full. Unlike most of the tools we use, the cup is considered a coven tool, being drunk from by all members and there for is not anointed with the witch's blood.

The wand, like the black knife, is an extension of the witch's hand. The wand is the chosen tool used for spells of prosperity, fertility, love, healing, creativity, and knowledge. In traditional Wicca, the wand is often made from hazel wood and is inscribed with magic symbols that can be traced to the Books of Solomon (similar to the Wiccan athame). This type of wand is often cut so that it measures from the elbow to the tip of the forefinger. Often the wand is associated with fire in the practice of Wicca, although there seems to be many who practice witchcraft and various forms of Wicca that associate this tool with the element of air.

〜

In our clan most witches will make several wands, choosing the wood for their magical qualities and shaping them into being. Most wands are fairly plain looking, while some witches do prefer to decorate their wands a little, the best wands are usually moderately designed to retain its natural look and feel. Many of our clan members have a variety of wands that include, but are not limited to, healing, protection, banishing, cursing and more. The size of the wand is entirely up to the practitioner. I often tell students that the wand, like any other tool, must be comfortable to hold, simple, yet pleasing to look upon.

Among the clan's members, our tools may vary somewhat depending on the witch's gender, status, and preference. We will now look at the implements of witchcraft that are not commonly found among Wiccan or neo-Pagan practitioners.

〜

Witch's implements need to always retain the qualities of nature, and as such, they should be somewhat natural in appearance, and when possible, shape as well. The *God Stone* and the *Hag Stone* are good examples of two objects coveted by witches for their natural qualities as well as their magical attributes. The god stone should be found in nature and cherished as a gift from the fey creatures and The Horned One himself. This tool may be gifted by another witch at initiation and should be received with great honor by the one that it is bestowed upon. The god stone is a phallic shaped rock, long and smooth in appearance representing the virility of the Horned One. Like the broom, the god stone is often consecrated with a female witch's vaginal fluid.

The hag stone is another object found in nature that is highly prized among witches. Usually, the hag stone is found in a river or near running water of some type. Hag stones are often small stones that have a naturally occurring hole bore into it so that the witch may peer through the stone and see the other side clearly. Hag stones should be sanctified under the full moon and fed with running water to activate its powers properly.

The dolmen is a large or semi-large flat stone used by our clan members as an altar. The original dolmen was used by Celtic tribes to create an entrance way into ancestral burial mounds. These entrance ways were portals of sorts into and out of the underworld realm of the fey spirits and the ancestral kin. During the burning times, we believe that most witches used the hearthstone as their dolmen /altar. With the fireplace set behind the hearthstone, this would make the perfect place to brew potions in the cauldron and perform spells without drawing much attention to one by the locals.

With the dolmen directly on the ground, a strong connection is forged with the spirits of the land, the genii loci, and the fey creatures of the landscape. The witch may also bring his or her dolmen inside to connect with the powers of the earth for spells and ritual. Some witches have taken to setting their dolmen on top of two or three other stones as the ancient Celtic peoples did. We see the dolmen as a type of household spirit, a guardian of the homestead. It is an earthen spirit that is consecrated and empowered by the witch. We mark the date that our dolmen is consecrated and then we re-consecrate it each year around the same date. We feel that it is best to do the dedication under the dark moon, anointing it in a bloodletting ritual or by anointing it with the *Blood of the Red Rose* or *Red Dragon*.

Like most tools of witchcraft, the dolmen is both magickal and practical. Since it is flat (or rather flattish usually), it makes a good surface for the witch to work his or her rites of sorcery upon. Using chalk, one may draw sigils upon the altar stone that can easily be washed away with a little water or by the rain itself. Candle wax also comes off the stone with little effort making it a perfect altar for candle magick. The dolmen is solid and absorbs heat as well as liquid. This means that the heat from a thurible will not leave marks on the altar and any wine or water spilled from the chalice will not damage it as it might with a wooden altar.

The dolmen is considered to be both feminine and masculine. In its feminine aspect, it aligns us with the energy of the earth and the realm of Falias. We also use the dolmen to align with the Blacksmith God, seeing the dolmen as a sort of anvil that we use to forge magick. You can see here that the dolmen is both the stone of Fal, linking us to Falias, but also the anvil of the gods, linking us to Findias.

The cauldron is a classic tool used in witchcraft. In Celtic myth, many deities of the Tuatha had magical cauldrons. The cauldron in witchcraft is a symbol of regeneration holding within it the powers of birth, death, and rebirth. The cauldron is the womb of the Goddess, and as such, it is the vessel of life that spirits spring forth from into the world of flesh. The cauldron is a melting pot of sorts, a brew of ancestral memory. We witches believe that the souls of the departed rise up through the cauldron to become incarnate once more. This is in reference to the souls that often reside in the underworld waiting to be stirred and summoned forth into the material world again.

When thinking of the cauldron this way and more importantly when using it in magick, the witch must remember that the cauldron is a portal! We can use the cauldron to summon forth spirits when needed as they can ascend up through the cauldron. When looking at the cauldron in this way, one can summarize that the portal works both ways. Not only can a witch conjure magick up through the cauldron, but he or she may also use the cauldron as a portal to direct the flow of energy onto the astral plane or to affect the realms of the underworld. By following the laws of magic in regards to witchcraft operations, this process can result in physical manifestation if the witch has the fundamental understanding of how it all works.

The cauldron as a tool of magick can be used to make water based potions and philters. It can also be used for the art of hydromancy under the full or dark moon. By adding small pebbles or sand into the bottom of the cauldron, the witch may use the vessel for candle magick or for burning magical incense. The cauldron is also perfect for petition magick. The burning slips of paper turn to ash in the cauldron sending your spells to the underworld where they churn in the womb of the Goddess.

〜

The bone knife is used by witches in our clan to represent the ancestors, the Horned Man and the Blood Mother. The bone knife is a personal tool that each witch makes or finds for use in sorcery and necromancy. The knife must have a handle that is made from bone, horn or antler (wood may be used if desired but is less effective in my opinion). The blade of the bone knife is always sharp so that it may be used to cut cords, herbs and other things as needed. The bone knife is considered a tool that links the witch to the ancestors and carries within it the vibration of the under-world, or the death current.

Some witches may choose not to use a bone knife at all, using the shelg instead, or red handled knife in its place. Either knife is acceptable and serves similar functions. The red knife (shelg) has already been discussed in chapter two, so I will not repeat that information here.

⌒

When a witch in our clan reaches the final initiation, they are allowed to use a staff, stang or cane as an implement of magick as well as a symbol of their mastery in the craft. The magister or magistra will choose one of these tools and one only. Just as there are tools and symbols that are specif-ic to the magistra, the stang is a tool used to represent the Horned God and should be used by the magister only. The magister may have his choice of any three mentioned tools, while the magistra may choose to carry a staff or cane.

These three tools, like most, serve a practical use as well as having magickal uses. First off, the staff, stang, and cane are used to find and keep balance during the ritual. In this way, it serves as a walking stick imparting stability and an even flow of energy. These three tools are also used for protection when walking in the woods; this is meant to imply physical protection from man or beast if needed. Also, these tools serve to protect the witch from astral nasties by beating the bounds as they walk. In this function, you may say that the staff, stang, and cane are not just symbols, but may be considered a type of weapon for the warrior that dwells inside the heart and mind of the initiate.

As just mentioned above, these three tools may be used to banish hostile spirits if needed. These include disincarnate souls, elementals, astral creatures, shades, fey beings and possibly thought forms. This is done by beating the bounds; walking through the area in question while stomping the ground with the pommel of your tool and chanting a spell of banishment or protection. You may also ward your home in this way by walking the perimeter of your property or working area repeating a charm of warding while beating the bounds. This creates an astral barrier giving some protections for a short time. This is part of the reason why the staff, stang or cane has an iron nail driven into its base. Iron, as the metal of Mars, is known for its ability to add force and is thus used for protection and banishment by witches.

These three tools are usually created by the student or gifted by one's teacher at some point during the second degree. Training with them is usually begun shortly after so that the student has a short period to bond with his or her implement properly.

The staff is to be made equal in height to the witch who will wield it. At the appropriate places, the staff is marked with sigils that line up with specific power points on the witch's body. These sigils are usually solar in origin for male witches and lunar-oriented for female practitioners. When the staff is made correctly, it becomes an astral double of the practitioner, similar to how the wand becomes an extension of the astral hand.

Once the staff has been marked it is then decorated to fit the witch. This is often done by hanging or fastening fetishes for

the witch'ss familiars or totems from the shaft, or by placing symbolic items that hold meaning to that practitioner
someplace upon the tool. Whether you choose to wield a
staff, stang or cane, it should be designed to reflect the personality of the user. The witch must forge a bond with this
tool just like any other; your spirit must touch the spirit that
dwells inside the tool. Staffs are often decorated and consecrated on either a Saturday, Sunday or Monday for their
planetary associations.

While the staff represents the Sun God or Moon Goddess,
the stang represents the *Witch Father*, sometimes referred to
as Old Horny. The stang resembles a pitchfork and in olden
days was often made from a pitchfork having the middle
tine cut off leaving only a stub. Another way to fashion a
stang is to use real deer antlers or the horns of a bull or goat
as the top of the stang. If this is the case, the top of the stang
doesn't necessarily need to be a V or U shape. The antlers
or horns are more than enough sufficient to represent the
Horned One.

My personal stang is of the last type, having the antlers of a
fallen deer as the god symbol. I use my stang as a walking
record of my life in witchcraft, the major events and the
initiates I have elevated are represented on my stangs shaft. I
have painted the initials of my third-degree students on my
tool and then tied items to hang from the shaft that sym-
bolizes those initiates. I also have personal symbols on my
stang to represent me; a string of malachite with bells, some
crow feathers and my spirit bag filled with power items.
Each of these items holds a memory of great meaning to me
adding to the power of the tool.

Many witches use the stang to connect with the fire in the
earth's core or to tap into ley lines pulling the energy up

into the surface for magical use. The magister or magistra connects to the serpent or dragon energy of the earth's magma core by using the staff, stang or cane. The magister and magistra learn to draw up the serpent fire into the stang to be used in magick.

For us, we see the cauldron as the *Sacred Well*, the dolmen as the *Stone of Fal*, and the stang as the *World Tree*. It's planted into the ground for some rituals where it symbolically reaches down into the underworld like the roots of Bile. At the same time, the top reaches up into the sky like branches spreading out into the upper realms.

In this modern age of witchcraft, many of our initiates and elders have taken to using the cane or rod as their third-degree implement of power. The cane or rod is a smaller version of the staff and a larger version of the wand. The cane is used in the same manner as the staff and the stang, usually decorated with images of totems or mythic creatures to which the magister or magistra have attuned his or her energy.

The cane sometimes acts as a blasting rod; it's made from blackthorn wood and is used for cursing. The cane can also be likened to a scepter. Scepters date back to the times of the Egyptians and the Roman emperors who used it as a sign of power, much the way the cane represents the magister or magistra's authority in the coven.

12

To Sanctify the Tools

As with all things in witchcraft the true work begins on the inner plans, training the self in mind to complete one's goals is a basic step in personal development. Creating and sanctifying tools is no exception to this rule. Of course, the witch cannot focus solely on the inner planes, and thus the tools of the craft will help the witch to ground into the material world of form. Greater understanding of the tools can come only after knowing yourself and where your power truly comes from. Many tools of the craft lean on the side of simple, being unadorned or loosely adorned with objects to enhance their magical potency.

As the witch progresses through the ways of the art, they will sanctify and enchant a number of different tools and objects to hold their personal power or those energies of a powerful entity that they will make contact with. This, of course, depends on the tool or the object being created. Over time, the witch will, of course, find his or her own ways to sanctify and enchant an object, and so that which I present here is more of an idea that one may use as a stepping stone in their own development towards self-sufficiency.

To begin, I will give an example of how one might go about the process to sanctify small or medium sized objects. For this I will use the wand as the primary focus, of course, the words and preparation can be switched easily to sanctify any number of small tools or power objects. For us, the wand is a true witch's tool, linking its crafter to the realm of Elphame and the fey creatures of nature. In many ways, the tree from which the wand is cut becomes the witch's altar for a short time. The witch will need to walk in nature(possibly several times) listening deep inside of the self until he or she hears the songs of enchantment that spring forth from Elphame, the city beneath the trees. When the witch hears the songs of the pale people, he or she will let it guide them to the correct tree. It is now time to bond in spirit with the tree, making it an offering of one's blood given freely and purposely from the finger of Venus.

Much thought should be put into the wands use and creation. Trees such as oak, hazel, ash, birch, elder, and apple will be more helpful when used by the witch in sorcery that focuses on beneficial magick, while other trees such as yew, willow or thorn would be best used for specific magicks. It's now that the witch must focus on the purpose that the wand is being crafted for, meditating to see if its properties correspond to the witch's desires.

On a night when the moon is growing and in a positive sign of air or fire, cut a wand that will be used for beneficial magicks. If your wand's focus will be for negative workings, then it should be cut when the moon is decreasing and in a negative sign of water. A wand made for general magick

should be cut when the moon is exalted; this may be anytime between the waxing crescent and the gibbous phase.
Regardless of in which phase you will be cutting, you will
need to look at Mercury, making sure to cut the wand when
the moon is in a good aspect to this planet and not in a state
of retrograde. After the wand is cut, you will need to wrap
it up in a dark colored cloth and leave an offering to the
tree of milk, honey or blood. The wood needs to dry for 1-3
months before you can carve or shape it into being.

To sanctify a wand with beneficial energies, the witch will
need to do the following ritual outdoors in view of the
moon as it waxes (waning moon to empower a negative
wand). In either case, the witch will need to work in a secret
dark place. Over a charcoal of burning frankincense (myrrh
for its negative counterpart), the witch shall pass the wand
through the rising smoke so that it may be purified on all
sides. The desire here is to psychically connect with the
wand finishing this act of purification only when you feel it
is free of any malignancy. The witch will now need to wrap
their wand back up in its dark cloth and secure it in a secret
place for a short time.

On the night of the full moon and in the hour of mercury,
the witch shall light two white (or black for a negative tool)
candles for illumination. He or she will now unwrap the
wand and place it in the center of the dolmen inside of a
triangle formed from chalk. With intense concentration, the
witch now traces the lines of the triangle with the fingers
seeing each line coming to life with energy. With a burning
coal of frankincense, vervain and a pinch of salt begin to
circulate the triangle in a sunwise motion with your censer.

When the time is right ,the witch will hold up the wand and
speak directly to the tool saying:

Spirit of Elphame,
I greet thee who dwell's within this wood.
Spirit of my spirit, my kin through blood and bond.
I have heard your song that enchants the soul,
calling to me from the great city of the dead that lays
hidden deep beneath the soil.

The witch will now anoint the wand with oil, their breath and a drop of their essence taken from the finger of Mercury. After, the witch shall speak again:

From I to thee, I give life; I give breath.
From I to thee, I give life; I give blood.
From you to me, and me to you,
A sacred trust, a hallowed tool.
My blood to thee, our spirits bind,
one in body, and one in mind.

Extinguish the candles and in the dark of night feel the power of the spirit that has been brought forth into the sanctified tool.

All of the witch's tools have a spirit and a fate of their own. All tools of the crafter have a purpose and often function both magickally and practically. Many of our tools are marked in blood. This is done so that the spirit of the witch can reach out touching the spirit of the tool. The two spirits then mingle and bond together forming a partnership that is ripe for magick.

13

Feasting from the Black Cauldron

What happens during the sabbat ritual in the physical world is but a reflection of that which is taking place in the hidden realm of the otherworld. The turning of the season's changes in more dramatic fashion when witnessed in the inner world rather than the slow progression we experience here on the earthly plane. When the sabbat rite reaches its zenith, and the otherworld is peaking with chaos and change, the gateway of that Sabbat's path is flung open, and the true sabbat is realized. The power that rushes into the world is felt in the witch's heart and seen with anointed eye, just as it is felt on the skin and seen in the landscape.

The sabbat seasons are nourished by the black cauldron of the underworld realm. Through the operations of ceremony which are both physical and psychic, the witch is fed with the powers of the Horned Lord and the Dark Lady. One may say that this cauldron of Elphame is a cornucopia of abundance in the paradisical world where all things are fed and thus given sustenance and continuation. This vessel is also the *Black Cauldron of Souls*, bubbling with essence, where the ancestors gain strength, waiting to rise in physical form once more.

All witches seem to practice their sabbat rites differently. There are some clans who celebrate four sabbats, while other clans celebrate none at all. Some witches celebrate specific days on the calendar year in respect to certain deities; these days then become recognized as that clan's sabbat cycle. My friend Orius practices in a clan that celebrates five such sabbats. To gain a better understanding of the sabbat cycle, we will stick with simplicity here and examine those days with which most witches are familiar.

The classic sabbat rituals are eight in number. The witch begins to truly understand these rites by learning the hidden cycles of the terrestrial lands, the celestial heavens, and the inner cycles of Tir Andromain and Magh Mor. Since there are already dozens upon dozens of books written in regards to the witch's sabbats seen as a fertility cult marking the changing of the seasons and the agricultural year, we will not repeat this info here, only mentioning it in a few passages as points of interest. To begin, we shall examine the cycles of the heavenly bodies of the celestial realm as they correspond to the astral tides and the entities of the underworld. It's important for the witch to recognize what is happening above them as well as what is happening in the secret world during the sabbat cycle.

We believe that the Celtic sabbat cycles followed the movement of the stars, the short journey of the moon, and the long journey of the sun on the grand scale of the macrocosm. The sabbats also coincide with the elemental or, seasonal changes of the wheel, the microcosm. Some believe that the original Celtic calendars were drawn according to the moon phases, and this may be the reason that the Celts worshiped 13 months as opposed to the 12-month calendars of today. The Celts celebrated Samhain as a three day month that marked the beginning of the New Year. The Celts at some point may have switched to the passage of the sun to mark their calendar days as most ancient civilizations found the sun to be more reliable in its timing, opposed to the erratic ever changing pattern of the moon.

Looking at things on the grand scale, our planet tilts during the summer towards the sun. This makes somewhat of an illusion as we view the midsummer sun. It appears that the sun is rising higher into the sky, but it is in fact due to the earth's tilting nature. The opposite happens during winter. As the earth tilts farther back, the sun appears to lower and the days begin to shorten.

This "tilt" or angle changes throughout the year as the planet rotates around the sun. The Earth's northern side (hemisphere) receives a large amount of sunlight, but six months later when the earth has rotated to the other side of the sun and tilting away from it, the other side of the planet is now receiving the sun's strength.

When the sun reaches its zenith, its highest point in the heavens, this is the time of the Summer Solstice. When the sun drops to the nadir, its lowest point, we call this the Winter Solstice. If one were to look at the time in between the two solstices, you would find the Equinoxes. Equinox, meaning equal or balance, are the two times of the year when we find light and darkness in harmony with one another. We find twelve hours of daytime and twelve hours of nighttime.

Astrological Pattern of the Major Sabbats :

Samhain= 15 degrees of Scorpio
Imbolc= 15 degrees of Aquarius
Beltane= 15 degrees of Taurus
LugŠassadh= 15 degrees of Leo

Samhain, a festival of the dead, dedicated to our ancestors is ruled by Scorpio the sign of death, sex, and regeneration. Beltane, the polarity of Samhain, is ruled by Taurus, the polarity of Scorpio. Beltane is the ritual of life, birth, and sacred union. We enter true Samhain when the sun reaches 15 degrees of Scorpio. True Beltane, is when the sun reaches 15 degrees Taurus. By studying this, we find that these two celebrations are exactly 6 months apart on the wheel by measurement of degree.

Samhain, October 31-Nov. 7th in 15 degrees of Scorpio
Beltane, April 30-May 7th in 15 degrees of Taurus

Sabbat: Samhain - Polarity - Beltane
Sign: Scorpio - Polarity- Taurus

Imbolc, the celebration of light returning from the darkness, is ruled over by Aquarius, the water bearer who ushers in the early spring. Lughnassadh, the polarity of Imbolc, is ruled over by Leo, the polarity of Aquarius. Lughnassadh is the celebration of darkness returning to take over the light. We enter true Imbolc when the sun reaches 15 degrees of Aquarius. True Lughnassadh, is when the sun reaches 15 degrees of Leo. Again, by studying these two celebrations, we find that they are exactly 6 months apart on the wheel by measurement and degree.

Imbolc, February 1⁻7th in 15 degrees of Aquarius
LugŠassadh, August 1-7th in 15 degrees of Leo

Sabbat: Imbolc- Polarity- LugŠassadh
Sign: Aquarius- Polarity- Leo

These sabbat rituals correspond as pathways to the Celtic otherworld. At Samhain and Imbolc, the dark season pathways leading to Tir Andromain, the Celtic underworld are opening (Samhain) and closing (Imbolc). This opening of the door at Samhain signals the beginning of the dark season, while Imbolc signals the return of light as the door to the underworld begins to shut.

At Beltane and Lughnassadh, the light season pathways leading to Magh Mor, the Celtic Upper world are opening (Beltane) and closing (Lughnassadh). This opening of the door at Beltane signals the beginning of the light season, while Lughnassadh signals the return of the shadow as the door to the Upper world shuts.

Astrological Pattern of the Minor Sabbats:

Winter Solstice = 0 degrees of Capricorn
Spring Equinox = 0 degrees of Aries
Summer Solstice = 0 degrees of Cancer
Autumn Equinox = 0 degrees of Libra

The Winter Solstice, a celebration of the sun in its nadir, is ruled over by Capricorn, the sign of restriction, laws, and rules. The Summer Solstice, the polarity of Yule, is ruled over by Cancer, the polarity of Capricorn. Summer Solstice is a celebration of the sun in its zenith while the sign Cancer marks this as a time of fertility, family and high emotions. We enter true Winter Solstice when the sun reaches 0 degrees of Capricorn. True Summer Solstice, is when the sun reaches 0 degrees of Cancer. Looking at these two celebrations side by side, we find that they are exactly 6 months apart on the wheel by measurement and degree.

Winter Solstice, between 19-25th of December
in 0 degrees of Capricorn

Summer Solstice, between 19-25th of June
in 0 degrees of Cancer

Sabbat: Winter Solstice - Polarity - Summer Solstice
Sign: Capricorn- Polarity- Cancer

The Spring Equinox is a celebration of the balance of light in the east, ruled over by Aries, the sign of physical energy and leadership. The Autumn Equinox, the polarity of Ostara (Spring Equinox), is ruled over by Libra, the polarity of Aries. The Autumn Equinox is also a celebration of the balance of light but in the west. Libra is a sign of peace, tranquility, and fairness. We enter the true Spring Equinox when the sun reaches 0 degrees of Aries. True Autumn Equinox, is when the sun enters 0 degrees of Libra. Again, looking at these two celebrations side by side, we find that they are exactly 6 months apart on the wheel by measurement and degree.

Spring Equinox, between 19-25th of March
in 0 degrees of Aries

Autumn Equinox, between 19-25th of Sept
in 0 degrees of Libra

Sabbat: Spring Equinox- Polarity -Autumn Equinox
Sign: Aries- Polarity- Libra

Like the major sabbats, these minor rituals also correspond
as pathways to the Celtic otherworld. At the Winter Solstice,
we reach the halfway point of the dark season. The door to
the underworld which began to open at Samhain is now
thrown wide open at the Winter Solstice. We are also lined
up with the realm of Falias. At the Spring Equinox, we reach
a balance point between light and dark, upper world and
underworld. Here the door to the realm of Gorias opens up
before us.

At the Summer Solstice, we reach the halfway point of the
light season. The door to the upper world which began to
open at Beltane is now thrown wide open at the Summer
Solstice. We are also in alignment with the realm of Findias.
At the Autumn Equinox, we reach a balance point again
between light and dark, upper world and underworld. Here
the door to the realm of Morias opens before us.

It seems that the Celtic calendar had two primary points of
focus, Samhain, and Beltane; the dark half and light half of
the year. Here we find that Samhain marked the beginning
of the dark season when we are soaked in the energies of the
underworld, and that Beltane marked the season of light,
a time that we are immersed in the energies of the upper
world.

When the sun reaches the zenith, we are exposed to more
sunlight than at any other time of the year. This is celebrated

as a time of great health and joy as the sun is strong and the world is vibrant, blooming with life. The doors to the upper world begin to open at Beltane, marking the beginning of the *light* cycle. At the Summer Solstice, when the sun reaches the zenith, the door is thrown wide open. Lughnassadh then marks the time that this door begins to shut again until we reach the Autumn Equinox when the door is fully closed for a brief time, and we find a balance point between the upper and lower realms.

The exact opposite happens at the Winter Solstice. When the sun falls to its lowest point, the nadir, we are exposed to more darkness than at any other time during the year. This is celebrated as a time of rest and comfort as we focus our energies inward to hearth and home. The lands are cold during this time, and vegetation is hibernating, resting for the coming year. It's at this time of long darkness that the door to the underworld is thrown wide open. This door begins to open at Samhain, marking the beginning of the *dark* cycle. At the Winter Solstice with the sun in its nadir, the door to the underworld is fully open. Imbolc marks the time that this door begins to shut, becoming fully closed at the Spring Equinox when once again we find a short-lived balance between the two extremes of the upper and lower worlds.

Winter Solstice

At the Winter Solstice, with the sun in its nadir and the door to the underworld thrown open, we gather to celebrate the rebirth of the Horned God. Our altar faces the northern direction at midwinter to align with the energies of the sun as it soaks in the energies of Capricorn. We decorate the working space and the stang with some of the following herbs; holly leaves and berries, cinnamon sticks, oak leaves, bay leaves, mistletoe, sandalwood, pine/pine cones, juniper and juniper berries, fir, birch bark, wintergreen, ivy vines, elder, orris (iris) root, ash and rowan leaves. For this ritual, we often call upon Bran and Branwen. Other gods and goddesses of Alban Arthen include the Dagda, Herne, and Bridhe. We also make an homage to Finvarra and his wife Oonach of the sidh.

Our clan's pathworking for Mid-Winter uses the symbolism of The Dark Goddess as she stirs the cauldron of spirits. The Horned God is reborn as a youth rising from the black underworld cauldron in the form of a wraith spirit. The Horned God is not completely in this world, nor is he in the underworld per say. The Horned One rides the veil of *Terra Umbrae* between the worlds becoming more and more tangible the closer we get to Imbolc. In this sabbat cycle, the Horned God is his most human in appearance. While some clans see the god as a large black goat during this solstice, we see him as a young man bearing very small goat horns upon his head, an obvious link to the sign of Capricorn (ruler of the Winter Solstice) whose symbol is the goat. The goat is one of the Horned Master's emanations as well as one of his totemic animals. The god is often seen nude, symbolizing his newness to the world and his freedom of spirit.

Imbolc

When we reach Imbolc, the altar is still facing to the north (it may be turned slightly to the northeastern horizon) so that we align with the powers of Aquarius, the water bearer. The door to the underworld is starting to close now. Some of the herbs gathered for this sabbat are; angelica, bay leaves, benzoin, coltsfoot, heather, myrrh and crocus among others. During this ritual, we most often call upon Arianrhod and Herne, but we do honor other Celtic deities as well, such as- Epona, Bridhe, Arawn and fey creatures such as Blodeuwedd and Aine, Fairy Queen of the Moon.

For our pathworking for Imbolc we see the face of the Dark Goddess in the sky as she wears the stars like a crown of light upon her head. The Horned Lord is now made flesh; his body has become muscular and strong. The small horns just a month ago are now fully grown goat horns with a candle of blazing light resting upon his head. You can see his cloven feet from under his simple white garment. The goat here is the totemic animal of Imbolc whose milk was used to feed the tribes and fill the chalice.

Spring Equinox

At the Equinox of Spring, the doors to the upper and lower realms shut temporarily. Our altar faces to the eastern quarter now so that we may feel the embrace of Aries, the Ram of Spring. We use some of the following plants to decorate the working space and the stang; cinquefoil, dandelion flowers, dogwood, marjoram, meadowsweet, thyme, tansy, mint, tulips, daffodils, and narcissus. For this ritual we often call upon Rhiannon and Cernunnos, but also Danu and the Green Man as the spirit of the vegetation are honored. We venerate the fey King Ossian and his fairy Queen Neve gifting them to bless the spring.

Our pathworking for Spring Equinox focuses on this being the time of the Veiled Goddess who bears the responsibility of closing the seams between the worlds sealing their doors shut. We now bask for a moment in the rays of the eastern city, Gorias. The Horned One now wears the mask of the ram, another of his totemic animals and an obvious nod to the sign Aries (ruler of the Spring Equinox) whose symbol is the ram. The god with his black ram horns has grown a short beard and has a chest covered in fur. His shoulders are wider, and he has grown to his full height.

Beltane

Beltane arrives in May, and with it, the sun enters Taurus. The door to the upper world is opened marking the beginning of the light half of the year. The altar faces south (or southeast) to draw in the Taurus energies for the ritual. Herbs gathered for Beltane are hawthorn, ivy vines, white rose, rowan, sorrel leaves, fern, hazelwood and apple leaves or fruit. During this ritual, we most often call upon Danu and Belannos. Other deities include- Rhiannon, Cernunnos, the Dagda, Queen Medb and all of the fey creatures under the mound. We always pay special attention to the Dryads and Hama Dryads at this time of early summer. The fey creatures are most active between the times of May and June. Offerings to these spirits should be made in accordance with the changing flora and fauna.

For our Beltane pathworking the Dark Goddess is busy stirring the spirits of the black cauldron, many of whom will be conceived in the physical world during this cycle of erotic pleasure for the continuation of life here in the physical realm. The White Queen is busy threading new life on the web of fate to be played out over the course of each spirits destiny. The Horned Lord has shed his horns more, now taking on the form of the Bull God. Beltane aligns with the energies of Taurus, the sign of fertility and abundance. In this emanation, the Horned Master is the King of the Greenwood Land, a lustful god who resides over rituals of ecstasy and pleasure. He is seen as a huge man of powerful build with large bull horns atop his head. Sometimes the Horned God is seen wearing a simple dark green or white robe, while other times he is seen nude with an erect phallus.

Summer Solstice

During the Summer Solstice, with the sun at its zenith and the door to the upper world thrown wide open, the spirits of the mighty dead descend upon the earthly realm with all of their splendor and might. We stand facing the southern direction to connect with the energies of Cancer and the blazing hot sun. The altar and stang are both decorated with some of the following; chamomile, elderflower, parsley, honeysuckle, fennel, lavender, mistletoe, mandrake, yarrow, strawberries, raspberries, nasturtiums, red roses, St. JoŠ's wort and vervain. During this sabbat, we call upon Bridhe and Cernunnos, as well as Danu, Dagda, and Manannan. During the Mid-Summer ritual, we also praise the fey folk of the Sidhe making offerings to the nymphs and their forest dwelling brethren.

For our Summer Solstice pathworking the Blood Mother is active during this time, symbolized by the red rose which is prominent upon our altar stone. The great dragon rises from the earth spreading its wings, slowly casting the shadow of the coming dark season. Soon the rose will begin to wither a little more each day until eventually the door of the underworld reopens again in October. During the Summer Solstice, the Horned God is envisioned with large bull horns blazing with the fire of the sun itself. This is a time when the solar deities and the spirits of the sky realm are most active. The earth and its inhabitants are in great health as the landscape around us is in full bloom and beauty.

Lughnassadh

When Lughnassadh arrives, the door to the upper world will begin to close. Our altar faces the southern (or southwestern) direction so that we may absorb the energies of Leo, the lion. Our working space and our stang are both decorated with the following herbs; frankincense, heather flowers, mistletoe, sage, oak leaves, oats, grains, and sun-flowers. The deities for this ritual are Lugh and Cerridwen. Other deities we honor are Macha, Bridhe, Cernunnos, the Dagda, and Medb. During the Lughnassadh sabbat, we honor the merry dancer, Fin Chlis as well as Finnine, the White Lady and sister of Aine.

Our pathworking for Lughnassadh sees the shadow of the dragon's wings spreading a little more each day as the sun slowly loses its vitality. We look to the lands to determine what the fall harvest has brought. If it has been a good harvest, the magistra shall be as Cerridwen, dressed in white and carrying the fruits of the fall with her in a basket. If the fall harvest has yielded little or the crops, have been blighted then the magistra shall be like Graidwen, dressed in black with a painted face and veil. With a sickle in hand, she enters the witch's ring in silence. The Horned Master now bears the antlers of the stag, another one of his sacred totems. The signs of his aging show as his muscular phy-sique begin to fade, and his skin begins to wrinkle slightly.

Autumn Equinox

At the Equinox of Autumn with the sun still decreasing, we enter into Libra, the sign of balance. We now face the west-ern direction, home of the ancestors and the greatest of har-vests. We bring some of these herbs to the sabbat; acorns, oak leaves, marigolds (calendula), milkweed, myrrh, pump-kins, gourds, squash, passionflower, sage, Solomon's seal and blessed thistle. The deities of the fall ritual are Mabon and Modron, but also Bran and Branwen, the Dagda, Lugh and the fey creature Saba as well as her lover Finn.

For our Autumn Equinox pathworking the Veiled Goddess again seals the doors between the upper and lower realms as we take rest and solace in the western city, Morias. The

Horned Lord's face is almost unseen from under the hood of his heavy cloak, all except for his massive antlers which have moss growing from their tines. His hands are wrinkled, and his fingernails are long as he grasps his staff.

Samhain

Samhain arrives in October, and with it, the sun enters the sign of Scorpio. The doors to the underworld begin to open up once more signaling the start of the dark season. Our altar faces north (or North West), and our space is decorated with the following; apple leaves and wood, pomegranates, gourds, squash, maize, grain, vervain, mugwort, and wormwood. The deities we use for Samhain are the Morrighan and the Dagda, but also Cerridwen, Cernunnos, Badb and the host of fey that ride out from the mound to take part in the wild hunt.

Our pathworking for Samhain has the Veiled Goddess lifting the veil between the worlds once more; the Dark Goddess slowly stirs her underworld cauldron awaiting new souls. The Horned God removes his hood showing his skeletal face still with huge antlers spreading out and up. The Horned Master is now the Lord of Death who will lead the host on their wild hunt. With his black robes and hellhounds, he leads those souls harvested through the gate of death and into the underworld where they will find transformation once again and rest among their ancestors.

14

Clan Formulary

The following is a list of formulas that have been created by our clan members to use for many different occasions. I will start this section with incense recipes. The following formulas are meant to be burned on a red-hot coal. Each incense recipe is designed to be half powder and half ground. Making incense this way will help your incense burn a little longer. You may simply grind the herbs in a mortar and pestle until they are ground up nice and small. Then take about half out and continue to grind the remaining herbs until the rest is powdered. Once this is done you simply mix the two together. You may decide to powder the whole thing if you wish. Spell powders can be used to dress candles or sigils. However, when used as incense, the powdered formula will burn much faster because of its fine texture .

When creating a new formula, we instill upon our coven members to always have an odd number of components as opposed to even numbers. This rule, of course, can be broken if the formula is being enhanced with numerology.

We always use dried herbs, roots, leaves and flowers. To these we add resin chunks or resin powder and a few drops of oil. The resins and oils may be excluded or substituted if desired, but we do strongly suggest that at least one of each is added to the recipe unless otherwise stated.

The measurements for the following formulas are given in parts. This is an easy measurement system for making large or small quantities of incense. If you wanted to make a small batch of incense 1 part might equal 10z., while a half part would then obviously equal ½ oz. and so on. A large batch of incense would be made by using larger parts. For example- 6 oz. = 1 part, 3 oz. =1/2 part, 1 ½ oz. =1/4 part and so on. Regardless of its size, your incense will need to be jarred and labeled for future use. I recommend using glass jars with cork tops, not only do they look attractive and witchy, but the cork will also help to absorb moisture (if there is any). If you cannot find this type of jar, any canning jar, mason jar or airtight container will work. It is best to avoid plastic zip lock bags altogether. There may be times when you have no choice but to use plastic, in which case you will want to double bag the incense in zip lock bags and label them well.

Incense Formulas for Sorcery

The following recipes are formulas created and used by the clan for the rites of power and the arts of sorcery.

Earth Serpent Incense

1 part Pine
1 part Cedar
1 part Nettles
½ part Patchouli
½ part Dragons Blood resin
A pinch of Sulfur
2 drops of Cinnamon oil

Burn this incense when working with the serpent energy found in the ley lines of the earth. Earth serpent energies are usually conjured with the staff, stang or cane by the witch. This incense blend may also be burned at some sabbat rituals.

For Reversing Magick

1 part Mullein
1 part Rue
½ part Dragons Blood Resin

To reverse a spell or curse back upon its sender, you should begin by writing the person's name on a piece of paper. Now burn the paper in your cauldron. Collect the ashes and mix them with the herbs given above. Burn this formula as part of your candle, poppet or psychic magick.

Praesidium Maleficis Incense

1 part St. John's Wort
1 part Agrimony
1 part Solomon's seal
½ part Blue Cohosh
½ part White Copal resin

Burn this incense on a charcoal block anytime that you are in need of protection from another practitioner of the arts. St. John's wort has a long history of protecting those in need from witchcraft spells and may be burned by itself if desired. If you know the person working against you, write his or her name down on paper and anoint it with dragons blood oil by making an X across the name. Then place your black knife down on top of the name and circulate the whole paper with this incense.

Praesidium Incense
   1 part White Oak bark
   1 part Solomon's Seal
   1 part Nettles
   1 part Juniper
   2 pinches of Witches Salt
   1-3 drops Sage oil
   5 Rowan berries (substitute Hawthorn if needed)
   *Hair from your familiar (or hair from a very protective dog if needed)

Burn this incense in your home, making sure to fumigate every room. Repeat this fumigation as needed. This formula is for basic protection of a non-descript type. For protection from magick, sorcery or witchcraft, use the "Praesidium Maleficis" formula given above.

Witch's Lightning Incense
   1 part Oak Bark from a tree struck by lightning*
   1 part Bay Leaf
   1 ¼ part White Copal Resin
   1 ¼ part Golden Copal Resin
   5 drops of Frankincense oil (or Bay oil)

   *(another wood may be used if oak is not available, as long as it is lightning struck)

Use witch's lightning to add extra power to your spells. Use it to warn or scare an enemy. Witch's Lightning Incense will add a kick to your sorcery.

Fairy Blood Incense

1 part Red Rose Petals
1 part Dragons Blood resin
1/2 part Elderberries
1/2 part Hawthorn berries
1/2 part Rowan berries
1-2 drops of Juniper oil
1-3 drops of your Blood, taken from the finger of Venus

This formula makes the fey around you more active. This formula may be burned when petitioning the fey in magick, spell work or at the sabbat rites.

Divination Incense

1 part Damiana
1 part Lemon Grass
1 part Wormwood
½ part Vervain, Blue
½ part Poppy Seeds
½ part Orris Root powder
1 whole, Star Anise, ground
3 drops Opium Oil
3-5 drops of Mugwort Oil

Burn this incense anytime you are going to practice the mystical arts of divination.

Necromancy Formulas

These formulas are used for the ceremonies of necromancy and ancestor working.

For Calming Spirits

1 part Camphor (known to calm spirits)
1 part White Rose flowers
1 part Pine needles (or 1 drop Pine oil)
1 part Sweet Grass
½ part Valerian root, ground into a powder
½ part Angelica root, ground into a powder
1 drop of Lavender Oil

Use this recipe to calm active or restless spirits as needed. Camphor is known to calm spirits and can be burned by itself if desired

Necromancy Incense, To Arouse the Spirits

1 part Mullein
1 part Wormwood
½ part Myrrh resin
½ part Pomegranate seeds, dried and powdered
¼ part Black Copal resin
¼ part Graveyard Dirt
3 drops of Mugwort oil
3 drops of Sweet Red Wine
3 drops of your blood, taken from the finger of Venus

Burn this incense blend on a lit coal in a swinging censer. Circulate the energy by swinging the censer in the appropriate direction in accordance with the spirit being invoked. After the work is finished, burn the Necromancy Incense to

release the spirits while circulating the incense in the opposite direction as that you used to invoke.

Necromancy Incense- To Release the Spirits
1 part White Sage, ground and powdered
1 part Agrimony
1 part Dittany of Crete
½ part Rue
¼ part Acacia Powder
¼ part Vesta Powder
¼ part Camphor Powder
3 pinches of Sulfur*
3 pinches of Witches Salt

*(sulfur should not be burned by itself unless you are
trying to summon a spirit)

The Sabbat Formulas

*The formulas presented here are used for the sab-
bat rituals of the sun and the moon.*

White Goddess Incense
1 part Gardenia Flowers
1 part White Rose petals
½ part White Sandalwood
½ part White Birch bark
½ part Willow bark
¼ part Ivy leaves
¼ part Meadowsweet
3 drops of Jasmine oil
3 drops of oil Sandalwood oil

Burn this incense when working with the White Goddess.

Dark Goddess Incense

1 part Violet flowers
1 part Vervain, blue
½ part Willow bark, (weeping if possible)
½ part Myrrh Resin
½ Mugwort
½ part Blackberry leaves
¼ part Valerian powder
1 drops of Lilac Oil
3 drops Neroli oil

Burn this incense when working with the Dark Goddess.

Red God Incense

1 part Mandrake
½ part Frankincense resin
½ part Golden Copal resin (Substitute Amber resin if needed)
½ Hazel Wood
½ part Calendula
½ part Cinnamon
½ part Bay leaves
¼ part Sunflower petals
¼ part Coriander seeds
5 drops of Amber oil
1-3 drops of Blood, from a magister's "Sun finger"

This incense is burned when working with the energies of the Red God, Lord of the Anvil- who is known by many names. This incense draws upon the energies of the sun and the realm of Findias. You may burn this incense during the sabbat rites of the summer solstice or when crafting new working tools. The Red God goes by many names and wears many masks.

Horned God Incense

1 part Oak Moss
1 part Deerstongue
1 part Mistletoe
1 part Mandrake
1-3 drops Musk Oil

Burn this erotic earthy blend to invoke the witch father in ritual. Burn it for fertility and sex magick, or for lust and luck, or protection.

Blood Moon Incense

1 part Bloodroot
½ part Patchouli
½ part Dragons Blood Resin
¼ part Fox Glove
¼ part Black Cohosh
¼ Skullcap
¼ part Damiana
¼ Benzoin powder
3 drops of Blood, from the finger of Saturn

Burn this incense on the night of the Blood Moon or when working magick with the ancestors. The ingredients in this recipe are mostly associated with Pluto, Saturn, and Mars.

Samhain Incense

2 parts dried Pumpkin leaves
1 part Mugwort
1/2 part Rosemary
1/2 part Patchouli
1/2 part Vervain
1/4 part Wormwood
1/4 part Sage (optional) or Rue
1 pinch Garlic
1 pinch powdered animal bones (or blood from the coven member's Saturn finger)

Winter Solstice Incense

1 1/2 part Pine bark
1 part Holly leaves
1 part Oak leaves
1/2 part Cinnamon
1/2 part Juniper berries
3-5 drops Bayberry oil
1 pinch Mistletoe

Imbolc Incense

1 part Yarrow
1 part Cinnamon
1 part Blessed Thistle
1/2 part White Sage
1/4 part Motherwort
1/4 part Frankincense
1/4 part Rose leaves (or 3-5 crushed Rose hips)
1-3 drops Sandalwood oil
1 pinch of wheat, dried and ground

Spring Equinox Incense

1 part dried tulip flowers
1 part Garden Mint or Spearmint
1/2 part Hyacinth or Lavender flowers
1/2 part Meadowsweet or Fern
1/4 part Oak Moss or Lovage
1-3 drops of Mistletoe oil

Beltane Incense

1 part Fern
1 part Meadowsweet
1/2 part white Rose petals
1/4 part Lilac flowers
1-3 drops Lavender oil
4 Elder Berries-dried and crushed

Summer Solstice Incense

1 part red Rose Petals
1/2 part Oak leaves
1/2 part Holly leaves
1/2 part Yarrow
1/4 part Heather
1/4 part Dragon's Blood Resin
1/4 part Jasmine flowers
3 drops Strawberry oil
and a pinch of Mandrake root

Lughnassadh Incense

1 paert Sunflower leaves and petals
1 part Yarrow
1 part Milkweed leaves
1/2 part Nasturtium or Calendula flowers
1/4 part red Clover
5 Hazelnuts (or leaves) dried and ground
1 pinch of Cornmeal A small amount of Honey

Autumn Equinox Incense

1 part autumn leaves*
1 part Mullein
1/2 part Bittersweet or Meadowsweet
1/2 part Calendula flowers
1/2 part Yarrow
1/2 part Apple leaves
1/4 part Chamomile flowers
1/4 part Frankincense resin
1 splash of red wine
1-3 drops of Apple oil
1 pinch of Wheat

*As a base for this, gather up the fallen leaves from the garden, or you could use all oak or ash leaves if you desire. Make sure all leaves are completely dry. This should equal 1 part.

Magickal Oils

There are essentially two ways to make magical oil, the metaphysical way, which happens to be the simpler way to create magical oil and the witch's way.

First, let's look at the newer and more metaphysical way to make oil. Get carrier oil, such as apricot, almond or grape seed oil (I recommend jojoba oil personally). You will also need your essential oils and an empty bottle (preferably amber or cobalt colored) with a screw on top or glass cork. Simply, add your carrier oil into the empty container until it is almost full, and then add your essential oils with an eye dropper until you achieve your desired effect. Boom... you're done. Label it and place it in a dark, cool place for when you need it!

In order to make a hedge witch's oil, you will need an empty bottle, a carrier oil (same as before), **fresh or dried herbs,** cheese cloth, a wooden spoon and an airtight container (for resins you will need a saucepan). You may also wish to add essential oils at the end if desired....your choice.

In the large airtight container add your carrier oil. Next, take up your herbs; charge them with energy and add them into the oil one at a time. Once all of the herbs are soaking in the oil take your wooden spoon and begin to stir the mixture. At this point, you should begin a chant that is appropriate for the purpose of the oil. When this is finished, place the lid on the container and place it in a cool, dark place. You will need to let this sit for about two weeks, giving the oil time to soak up the scent of the herbs. Make sure to shake this a little bit every day while the herbs and oils are blending.

After the two week period, open the lid and smell the oil. If it isn't strong enough, you may decide to strain the oil and add another batch of herbs to the oil repeating the two-week process again. When the oil is to your liking, strain the oil and herbs through cheesecloth. Disregard the cheese cloth and the herbs. Now you will need to pour the oil into a clean bottle with a tight cap. Label the oil and store it away in your magical cabinet.

If the formula you are using calls for resins or tree barks you will need to boil the oil over a very low flame. Place your saucepan on the stove or over a campfire and add your carrier oil. Pick up your herbs, charge them with energy and add them to the oil. Slowly start to stir the oils. While doing this, you will need to chant a rune prepared ahead of time. Concentrate on the purpose of the magic oil as you chant and stir. Make sure to stir the oil in the direction that is most beneficial to the oils purpose.

Do not let the oil bubble! It should only simmer slightly-not cook. The resins should melt into the oil and will probably change the oils coloring slightly. When done, strain the oil and resins through cheese cloth. When the oil is cool to the touch, bottle it, label it and store it away in your magical cabinet. Disregard all of the leftover ingredients.

Altar Oil

    1 part Myrrh
    1 part Frankincense

These herbs have a very high vibration of energy. This formula is used by many witches as anointing oil at their sabbat rituals. Frankincense is fire and Myrrh is water, together they create temperance and contain within them the power of the hexagram. This formula must be heated so that the resins melt into the oil.

Fairy Flower Oil

1 part Lavender flowers
1 part Lilac flower
1 part Fern
½ part Tulip flowers
½ part Rose petals
¼ part Mint leaves
¼ part Lily of the Valley, flowers and leaves
¼ part Violet flowers

After the herbs are strained add:

1 drop of Thyme oil, or Bergamot oil

Use this to call on the Nymphs and other forest fey at sabbats. Use this oil for divination or to enchant someone with love magick. Fairy Flower oil is also used in the sabbat rituals of Beltane and the Summer Solstice when the power of the fey is at its peak.

Fairy Blood Oil

In a sauce pan, add:
1 part Dragons Blood resin
1/2 part Elderberries
1 part Red Rose Petals

When the resins and herbs have simmered and cooled, add the following:

1-2 drops of Juniper oil
1-2 drops of Geranium oil

Green Fairy Oil

In a container with an airtight lid, add:
1 part Mugwort leaves
1 part Green Sage leaves
1/2 part Lemon Grass

Let this mixture sit for about one week, strain the herbs through cheesecloth. discard the used herbs and pour the scented oil into another clean, airtight container. To this add:

1 part Wormwood herb (Artemisia)
1/2 part Mugwort leaves

Now, this mixture must sit for an additional two weeks in a dark, cool place. Again, this mixture is strained after the two weeks through clean cheesecloth. To this add:

1 drop of Sage oil
1-2 drops of Lemon Grass oil

Pour the finished product into clean amber bottles. Use Green Fairy oil when performing trans work, ancestral work, divination, clairvoyance or hedge crossing.

Ignis Oil

In a sauce pan, add:
1 part Dragons Blood resin (must be heated so that it melts)
½ part Oak bark
¼ part Allspice (or Cinnamon, your choice)

When the resins and herbs have simmered and cooled, add the following:

1 drop Clove oil (caustic)
1-2 drops Spearmint oil (caustic)

Use Ignis (fire) oil for spells that you want or need to materialize in a hurry. This oil can be used for spells of passion as well as protection.

Horned God Oil

1 part Oak moss
1/2 part Rowan Bark
1 pinch Mistletoe

Add the herbs to a container filled with grape seed oil. After this has been strained (about two weeks), add

1 drops Musk Oil
1 drop of Ambergris

Bottle this erotic smelling oil and wear it to invoke the witch father in ritual. Use it for fertility and sex magick, as well as for lust, luck, or protection.

Benedictio Oil

1 part Lavender flowers
1 part White Roses
½ part Vervain, blue
½ part Sage
½ part Cedar or Juniper
¼ part Chamomile flowers
1-2 drops Jasmine oil

Use this blessing oil to anoint your coven for ritual or dress a white candle with it to bless your home.

Oraculum Oil

1 part Mugwort
1 part Damiana
½ part Lemon Grass

Use Oraculum oil anytime you are working with divination, prophesying or doing oracle readings.

Corpore Sano Oil

3 drops Bergamot oil (or Rose oil)
2 drops Neroli oil 1-2 drops Frankincense oil

Corpore Sano is healthy body oil used to anoint the sick as well as candles and poppets in healing sorcery.

15

The Romances of Witchcraft

It was a few short weeks before the Spring Equinox of 2002. Our group had gathered at our coven mother's house and quickly realized that it would only be her and I attending the Sabbat. We took care of some other business that needed attending and then went to her kitchen to make our plans for the spring rite and a small feast for two. After deciding on the ritual changes that needed to be made, as well as our menu, she had come up with a brilliant idea! We would release back into the wild some small quails (birds) that she had been raising. She had kept them in a small cage in her back room and no longer wanted the daily chores of keeping them just for the tiny little eggs they produced. We decided that after the ritual we would throw them over the bank and watch them fly away.

The day of the ritual finally came. If anyone reading this has ever been to Upstate New York in March, they will know that the spring is just another name for mud! There are actually only three seasons in New York; there are roughly three months of summer and a super long winter, which is then followed by mud season. Trying to make it up her driveway in the middle of the *Mud Equinox* was no joke. My car was slipping and sliding all over the place, and I had to try the driveway several times before I was successful. Of course, when possible, we witches love to work outdoors. Our plans had been to perform the rite on the side of the hill not too far from her gardens. We decided to stick with the game plan and divide up the duties since there were only two of us present. I went outside to set up our working space, while she prepped the food for the celebration.

It was hot outside that day. You never know what to expect in New York. Some years during the Equinox we had snow. Usually, we had rain, but every once in a while, like that year; it was beautiful sunshine. However, the ground was muddy and very slippery. We stumbled all over the place as we cast the ring, performed our invocations and other ritual actions. It's always scary to see your magistra moving around the working area with a ritual knife not knowing if she is going to slip and impale you…..accidently of course. The sun was bright which made it very hard to see, let alone read anything written, and we ended up squinting through much of the day. Of course, there were also the mosquitos! It was bright and sunny which meant that the bugs were out and since it had been a long winter they seemed to be extra hungry. By the time the ritual was done, we had several large mosquito bites which resembled tumors all over our legs and arms.

Finally, the time had come for us to release the quails back to nature. We each took two quails in hand and moved to the edge of the bank. Our coven mother said a small blessing and we tossed the tiny birds into the air. In our minds, we had both envisioned a scene similar to something from a movie, complete with sappy music and a beautiful sunset. Instead, the birds fell to the ground by our feet and looked at us, as if saying "What the hell are you guys doing!" We both started to laugh as we tried to gently brush the little birdies over the bank so they could be on their marry way. Since they had never been out of their cage, they had no idea what to do and the thought of "being free" didn't compute in their pea sized brains.

Obviously, our ritual didn't go as planned. However, this is the way of nature. No two years are exactly the same and making plans for any sabbat should probably be a little tentative. We had a beautiful ritual planned, but instead, we ended up with a very messy, uncomfortable rite indeed. Before I had this experience, I had read a thousand Llewellyn[9] books which always described beautiful rituals under the full moon or the lovely bright sun. They talked about witches dancing, singing and making merry. They detailed rituals that sounded awe inspiring and left me longing to have similar celebrations myself. What these books don't tell you is that you usually can't see in the dark, so dancing usually means falling, tripping over branches and tree roots, or stepping on something sharp like twigs and the like. You might as well forget about reading from any kind of script in the dark and drinking from the chalice becomes a little game we like to call, "What's crawled inside the cup"….. yuck!

Working under the sun means you're going to burn, sweat and be blinded by the sun's mighty power. I have seen many witches leave an afternoon sabbat a little crispy and covered in mosquito bites. One time at a Pagan gathering in Pennsylvania I watched as the coven altar burst into

9   Llewellyn Worldwide, founded in 1901 is a widely known Pagan, Metaphysical, New Age publishing company located in Minnesota.

flames. It seems that the priestess wasn't paying attention and knocked over some lantern oil, which then caught on fire because of the candles she was using. Having a bonfire at ritual is always welcome, our coven loves it, but it can be more than a little hard to concentrate with smoke in your eyes, and chanting becomes impossible if you are choking and hacking on black fumes.

As witches, we love to perform our rites outside. Here in Florida however, it is boiling hot, to say the least. This doesn't mean we don't work our magicks outdoors. Sometimes we make sacrifices for our workings and being uncomfortable comes with the territory. If you can't leave your air conditioner for a few hours in order to get back to nature, then you probably shouldn't practice witchcraft. The way of the witch isn't about being comfortable; sometimes we need to get messy in order to accomplish our goals. To quote Mathew Fox:

"If you look closely at a tree you'll notice its knots and dead branches, just like our bodies. What we learn is that beauty and imperfection go together wonderfully."

In our minds, we all tend to romanticize the craft sometimes. However, the reality doesn't always match the romantic rituals we dream up and set out to perform. Nothing in nature is perfect, even if the books on your shelf tell you they are. As witches, we realize things just as Conrad Hall has said;

"There is a kind of beauty in imperfection."

Magickal Terminology

A

Adeptus- A Latin word meant to be used as one who has attained (mastered) a magickal degree or grade within a magickal order.

Alchemy- Originally meant to describe a magickal process by which one could transmute base materials (such as metals) into another form (such as gold or silver). Alchemy, however, can have several different meanings depending on the magical order that one is taught in.

Alpha- Alpha is a state of mind (brain wave pattern) that is desired for magick to be accomplished.

Alraun- A poppet made from the branches of a sacred tree. Similar to a Mandragore.

Amuletum- A Latin word used to describe an object empowered with magick. Meant to be carried on the person to gain the magickal effects it was created for.

Aphrodisiac- herbs (and other items) that can cause sexual arousal when eaten, drank or burned as incense.

Artifice- Artifice, meaning "artificial spirit" is used by witches and magicians to describe thought forms and elementals.

As the word implies, this is not a real or natural spirit, but rather one created through will power and ritual.

Archetype- Archetypes were originally coined by Dr. Jung to describe patterns of behavior in his patients. Archetypes represent different qualities in the human psyche. There are many archetypes to be found in Wiccan and witchcraft traditions. The archetypes of god and goddess exist within us all.

Averse- 1. An ill effect caused by magick.
  2. A feeling of opposition towards something or someone.

B

Baneful- To affect someone with, or be affected by harmful magick or a curse. Might also be used to imply the use of a poisonous substance such as an herb or powder.

Banishing- To drive away a person, spirit or situation with magick.

Betwixt- Meaning to be between or in-between to places or elements simultaneously.

Binding- A type of spell cast to restrict a person or spirit from performing certain acts.

Bi-location- This is a form of mind travel, similar to astral projection.

Black Knife- As the name implies, this is a blade used by witches with a black hilt for rituals and spells.

Blood of the Red Dragon- This is semen or ejaculate from a magister or male witch. Used in spell work and sorcery.

Blood of the Red Lion- The blood of a Magister or male witch, usually taken from one of his fingers for sorcery.

Blood of the Red Moon- The blood of a magistra or female witch, usually taken from one of her fingers for sorcery.

Blood of the Red Rose- This is menstrual blood or vaginal fluids from a magistra or a female witch. Used in spell work and sorcery.

C

Call- To call is another word for invocation. The witch would call or invoke a spirit for magickal means.

Charm- 1. A small object created for a magickal purpose. These are usually made from natural materials and are worn, carried or hung in the home.
2. Chanting a prepared verse in rhythmic form to raise energy.

Clairaudience- Latin meaning "clear hearing" or the ability to hear things that others cannot. This often includes hearing spirits, or voices from the past.

Clairsentience - Latin meaning "clear sensing" or the ability to feel things that others do not feel on an emotional level. This often includes empathy and the psychometric arts.

Clairvoyance- Latin meaning "clear seeing" or the ability to see things that others are not seeing. This often includes having visions of the past, present or future as well as seeing auras or spirits.

Conjuration- Calling a spirit, demon or angel by use of their sacred names.

Clout- To strike an object with another object in spell work, similar to a hammer stroke.

Covenant- 1. A group of witches that practice magick together.
2. To make a pact or promise

Cowan- Used to refer to the uninitiated or those people who are non-witches.

D

Daemon- Sometimes seen as *daimon*, both being Latinized versions of the Greek used to describe a number of super-natural beings. Some daemons were seen as benevolent while others were considered benign. Daemon is essentially another way of saying spirit or nature spirit. It became the root word for the later Christian word *demon*.

Devotion- A short ritual or prayer used to contact a spirit, ancestor or deity. Often this act is accompanied by an offer-ing of some type.

Devil- 1. A pre-Christian name used by some to describe the Horned God. Also known as *Old Hornie* or the *Horned One*. This name fell out of popularity with the rise of Christianity.
2. A Christian term used to describe the biblical Satan, an entity composed from Pagan deities as a way to bastardize their gods and nature spirits.

Devils Foot- This is a symbol with six spokes of equal length. Somewhat similar to a hexagram but made from straight lines as opposed to triangles. The devils foot is sometimes substituted with the Algis rune. Other names for the devils foot are- devils trident, druid's foot or witch's foot.

Dolmen- 1. A series of large stones used a monument for the dead. Dolmens were also used as an entrance to the underworld.
2. A large stone altar that rests upon the ground, the dolmen is seen as a tool of the earth as well as a type of anvil. The dolmen is also a type of hearthstone and household familiar.

Dowsing- The art of divination using a pendulum, water stick or dowsing rods to find lost items. These devices may also be used to answer simple yes or no questions as well.

E
Elder- In our clan an elder is a magister or magistra who has been practicing the craft for twenty plus years. They are held in respect by all other members for their knowledge and experience.

Elemental- 1. A type of spirit that is born of and composed of a specific element. This type of elemental resides in a specific plane of its elemental nature.
2. used by some to describe a thought form created by will power and ritual. This type of elemental is an artifice.

Elphame- Elphame is sometimes called the city under the tree, while other times it is called the realm of enchantment. This is a world/city in which the fey creatures reside under the rule of fey kings and queens.

Enchantment- A technique used in magick to empower an object or person with your desires. This can be accomplished in many ways.

Enochian- Channeled information that is sometimes called the language of the angels. The alphabet and other information were later used by the Golden Dawn where it was developed into complex ritual.

Evil Eye- A form of fascination or enchantment cast through the eyes. This type of enchantment is of the malefic variety. Sometimes the evil eye is called the *malocchio.*

*Evocation-*Evocation is a ritual process that calls a spirit to manifest in the physical world.

Exorcism- 1. A minor ritual used to cleanse objects or spaces from the influence of demons, elementals, shades and possibly others.
2. A Catholic ritual believed to cast out "evil," such as demons or devils that have taken up residence with a human host.

F
Familiar- 1. a type of animal that the witch has psychically bonded with through ritual.
2. a spirit that the witch conjures by invoking the Horned God. This spirit is bonded with the witch and helps him or her to cast spells and perform rituals.

Fascination- a type of enchantment that is often cast through the eyes. Some consider this to be a type of glamour.

Fetch- There a number of different terms used to describe the fetch. My original teaching was that the fetch is a spirit of a person or animal that is forced to serve the will of a witch by means of magical ritual. Another common and possibly more modern definition is that the fetch is a spirit double of a witch. A type of shadow self that connects the witch to the lower realms.

Fluid Condenser- A term coined by Sybil Leek to describe an herbal formula in which a substance concentrates energies for magick.

G

Genius Loci (sometimes Genius Loki)- This is the word used to describe a spirit or guardian of a place in the natural landscape.

Genii Loci- Similar to the *genius loci* but plural, referencing multiple guardian spirits that inhabit the same place in nature.

Genii Locorum- A singular spirit with a larger territory than a *genius loci*. A spirit or guardian that watches over multiple places.

Glamour- A type of illusion such as- making oneself become unnoticeable (invisible), appearing to be beautiful in the eyes of others or making yourself seem frightening to others when looked upon.

Goetia- 1. The Goetia refers to a form of sorcery in which one invokes angels and demons to work the will of a magician.

2. Refers to the medieval Grimoire, the Lesser Key of Solomon, a book based on low magick.

Grimoire- Grimoires are books of ritual magick. There are many Grimoires dating from medieval times to the modern era.

H

Hallow- Hallowing a space is to cleanse it and make it ready for ritual work or magick. Hallowing cleanses and makes a space sanctified.

Hexagram- The Hexagram (also Hexagon) is a six-pointed star that relates to the sun and the sphere of Tiphareth on the Tree of Life. The hexagram is often used in witchcraft and Wicca.

I

Infusion-An herbal preparation for medicine.

Invocation- Calling power from within to beseech a spirit or god. Invocation brings that which is inside out, without physical manifestation.

L

Loa- Spirits used for magick in the religions of Vodou and Santeria. Sometimes the Loa are used in Hoodoo magic depending on the practitioner.

Left Hand Path- an older term still used by some to define a witch or magician who works dark or black magick. The term black magick in itself is rarely used anymore as it is an oversimplification of true magick.

Ligature- When used in reference to magick, the ligature is a form of ceremonial binding.

M

Magick- Spelled with a K at the end to differentiate between stage "magic" and occult "magick."

Magistellus- A name or title given to a witch's familiar spirit.

Magister- Magister is a Latin word that translates as master or teacher. When used in the context of witchcraft, the magister is considered the master of the circle who teaches both initiates and non-initiates. In simple terms, the magister is an initiated male witch who leads a coven.

Magistra- The magistra, meaning *mistress*, is the female version of the magister. A magistra is an initiated female witch who leads a coven.

Magistrix- magistrix is a word used among witches when referring to an animal familiar.

Magnetism- This is used to describe a form of occult power or psychic ability in which a person's aura is very dynamic. This aura is what draws followers to them. This may be likened to the old saying – "like moths to a flame."

Magus- A word used to describe a magician of ceremonial magick.

*Manteia (*Also Mantia, Mancy or Manci) - Manteia is a word that means divining the future. This is can be accomplished by any number of divination practices.

N

Nigromantia (sometimes called Nekromanteia or Necromancy)- All three of these words refer to divining the future by means of the spirit realm. In ancient times this may have included the use of corpses or sacrificial animals.

Nemeton- A Nemeton is a sacred place in nature that is filled with ancestral memory.

O

Offering- Something that is given to appease or empower a spiritual force.

Occult- Occult is a Latin word meaning "secret." This is often used to define various (if not all) magickal lodges, temples and covens that practice oathbound material.

P

Pentacle- A ritual star that is used in the practice of magick. This symbol has many meanings and is used by many occult groups.

Pentagram- Like the Pentacle, however, this ritual star has a circle around it.

Planetary Hours- A list of hours associated with the seven classic planets used in astrology. This chart is used to choose the correct time to start a spell or ritual.

Poppet- Similar to a voodoo doll, the poppet is used by witches in the practice of sympathetic magic.

R

Rune/Runes- 1. Describing Norse symbols used in magick and divination.
  2. A rune is also another word for a chant or verbal spell.

S

Sabbat- These are the seasonal rituals of witchcraft based on the movement of the sun, the moon and earth's ever changing landscape.

Sacrifice- The word sacrifice often conjures images of the ritualistic killing of a human or animal; however, a sacrifice can be many things including the offering of food, drink, money or other items when given freely to a spirit.

Scrying- Scrying is a specific form of divination that produces visions. These include things such as mirrors, crystal balls, water and more.

Seal- A type of sigil.

Servitor- This is sometimes used to describe a fetch (servant type spirit), while other times it is used to mean a familiar spirit.

Serpens- Serpens (or Serpentes) is the Latin word for serpent or snake.

Shade- A shade is often considered to be the remnants of someone who has passed away. Shades are sometimes called shadow people and are encountered close to the place of their physical death.

Shelg- A red handled knife used for ceremonial bloodletting rituals or spells involving the use of blood.

Sigil- Sigils are symbols that are created to contain a mass amount of information at a quick glance. Sigils act like keys when used in magic or ritual. Once activated, they unlock the information contained inside.

Simple- Herbal remedies using a singular herbal component.

Singulum- Singulum is the name for an initiation cord in some traditions.

Sorcery- Sorcery is often defined as the casting of spells and magick.

Speculum- Alternative name for a crystal ball or black mirror.

Staff- The staff is a symbol of the highest ranking members of some clans and traditions of witchcraft.

Stang- The stang is a tool wielded by the magister of a coven. It is used to represent the Horned God and the World Tree. The stang is a staff that has deer horns mounted to its top or is carved in the shape of a Y. Some stangs are simply pitchforks with two or three tines.

T

Tincture- An infusion of herbs soaked in alcohol.

Theban- Magical script used by witches and others to write spells, secret messages and to inscribe objects. Theban can also be used to create sigils.

Tobby- A tobby is a mass of ugly knots that is created purposefully when performing knot magick.

U

Unguent- An unguent is a greasy substance such as a salve or ointment. Some unguents made by witches contain poisonous herbs, flower, roots or barks.

V

Vibrate- The vibrating of sacred names or words when performing an invocation.

Volt- Psychic link; hair, nails, clothing, fluids, blood…..

W

Wards or Warding- To protect one's home or property with magick.

Warlock- Thought to mean "*Traitor or Traitor against God.*"

Wicca- Wicca is a modern form of witchcraft or neo-paganism founded by Gerald Gardner.

Witch- One who practices witchcraft.

Witchery- Witcheries are abilities that manifest without the use of ritual or tools. Witcheries often simulate spell effects or psychic abilities.

Witchdom- The word witchdom is sometimes used to refer to the afterlife or sometimes as part of the witch's cosmology.

Wort- Wort is an English word meaning "herb."

Wraith- The word wraith is often used to describe a spirit or ghost that has a misty or translucent appearance. Sometimes the words phantom and wraith are used interchangeably.

Wraith Form- The projection of the witch's (or coven's) astral body.

Bibliography

Abusch, Tzvi. *Mesopotamian Witchcraft: Toward a History and Understanding of Babylonian Witchcraft Beliefs and Literature*. Leiden, Netherlands: Brill Styx, 2002.

Ashe, Geoffrey. *Mythology of the British Isles*. UK: Methuen, 1990.

Beyerl, Paul. *The Master Book of Herbalism*. Custer, Wash: Phoenix Publishing Inc., 1984.

Bonnechere, Pierre. *"Divination" In a Companion to Greek Religion*. Daniel Ogden, ed. West Sussex, UK: Wiley-Blackwell, 2010.

Buckland, Raymond. *Buckland's Complete Book of Witchcraft*. St. Paul, MN: Llewellyn Publications, 2002.

_____. *The Witch Book; The Encyclopedia of Witchcraft, Wicca, and Neo-Paganism*. Visible Ink Press, 2001.

Chumbley, Andrew D. *Azoetia: A Grimoire of the Sabbatic Craft*. UK: Xoanon, 1992.

Conley, Craig. *Magic Words: A Dictionary.* San Francisco: Red Wheel/Weiser, 2008.

Davies, Sioned, trans. *The Mabinogion.* UK: Oxford University Press, 2007.

Day, Christian. *The Witches' Book of the Dead.* San Francisco: Red Wheel/Weiser, 2011.

Deveraux, Paul. *Fairy Paths & Spirit Roads.* UK: Vega, 2003. Dillon, Myles. *Early Irish Literature.* Chicago: University of Chicago Press, 1948.

Flint, Valerie, and R. Gordon, G. Luck and D. Ogden. *Witchcraft and Magic in Europe. Vol.2, Ancient Greece and Rome.* London: The Athlone Press, 1999.

Fortune, Dion. *Psychic Self Defense.* San Francisco: Red Wheel/Weiser, 2001.

Fortune, Dion. Applied Aspects of the Occult. San Francisco; Red Wheel/Weiser, 2003.

Gimbutas, Marija. *The Gods and Goddesses of Old Europe7000-3500 B.C.* Los Angeles: University of California Press, 1974.

Ginzburg, Carlo and R. Rosenthal, trans. *Ecstasies: Deciphering the Witches Sabbath.* Chicago: The University of Chicago Press, 1991.

Glob, .P.V. *The Mound People: Bronze-Age Man Preserved.* UK: Faber and Faber, 1973.

Graves, Robert. *The White Goddess*. UK: Faber and Faber, 1948.

Gray, William. *The Rollright Ritual*. UK: Helios Books, 1975
.

Guiley, Rosemary Ellen, and T. Taylor. *The Encyclopedia of Ghosts and Spirits*. New York: Checkmark Books, 2007.

Hoke, Gary Lee. *Coven Of The Catta, Elders and History Unique Ritual Practices and Spells*. Lulu.com, 2011

Hopman, Ellen Evert. *Tree Medicine, Tree Magic*. Custer, Wash: Phoenix Publishing Inc., 1991.

Huson, Paul. *Mastering Witchcraft: A Practical Guide for Witches, Warlocks and Covens*. Bloomington, IN: iUniverse, Inc., 2006.

Jackson, Nigel Aldcroft. *Call of the Horned Piper*. UK: Capal Ban LTD, 1994.

Jones, Evan JoŠ, and Valiente, Doreen. *Witchcraft: A Tradition Renewed*. UK: Robert Hale, 1990.

_____. *The Roebuck in the Thicket: An Anthology of the Robert Cochrane Witchcraft Tradition*. UK: Capal Ban LTD, 2001.

Kieckhefer, Richard. *Forbidden Rites: A Necromancers Manual of the Fifteenth Century*. Stroud, UK: Sutton Publishing, 1997.

Leland, Charles Godfrey. *Aradia or the Gospel of the Witches*. Blain, WA Phoenix Publishing, 1998.

Mathers, S. Liddell MacGregor. *The Key of Solomon the King: Clavicula Salomonis. Weiser Books, 2000.*

Markale, Jean. *Woman of the Celts.* Rochester, Vt: Inner Traditions International, 1986.

Martello, Leo Louis. *Witchcraft: the Old Religion.* Secaucus, NJ: Carol Publishing Group, 1987.

Martin, Lois. *The History of Witchcraft.* Chartwell Books, 2009.

Paddon, Peter. *A Grimoire for Modern Cunning Folk: A Practical Guide to Witchcraft on the Crooked Path.* USA, Cal: Pendraig Publishing, 2011.

Pearson, Nigel. *Treading the Mill: Practical Craft Working in Modern Traditional Witchcraft.* UK: Capal Ban LTD, 2007.

Pennick, Nigel. *Operative Witchcraft.* UK: Lear Books, 2011.

Rabinowitz, Jacob. *The Rotting Goddess: The Origin of the Witch in Classical Antiquity.* Autonomedia, 1998.

Rankine, David. *The Complete Grimoire of Pope Honorius.* Avalonia, 2013.

Ryall, Rhiannon. *West Country Magic.* Custer, Wash: Phoenix Publishing Inc., 1989.

Stewart, R.J. *The Underworld Initiation.* Aquarian Press, 1985.

Summers, Montague. *History of Witchcraft and Demonology, Hardcover.* Bristol Park Books, 2010.

Valiente, Doreen. *Witchcraft for Tomorrow*. UK: Robert Hale, 1993.

_____. *Natural Magic*. Custer, Wash: Phoenix Publishing Inc, 1985.

_____. The Rebirth of Witchcraft. UK: Robert Hale, 2008.

About the Author

Amaranthus has been a practicing witch since the age of fifteen. The author has been a student of the occult practicing and teaching Witchcraft, Wicca, Hoodoo, Folk Magick, Ceremonial Magick, Astrology and Reiki for over twenty-five years. During the last few decades, he has been involved in nine different covens from various places in the United States.

Amaranthus draws from his extensive years of practice in various forms of the Occult, providing others an opportunity to learn from a Magister and clan elder. When not writing, the author often travels teaching and lecturing to those who will listen.